Vocabulary Power Plus
for the New SAT:
Vocabulary, Reading, and Writing Exercises for High Scores

Book One

By Daniel A. Reed

Edited by Paul Moliken

ISBN-10   1-58049-253-3
ISBN-13   978-1-58049-253-9

Revised March, 2006

PRESTWICK HOUSE, INC.
"Everything for the English Classroom!"

P.O. Box 658 • Clayton, DE 19938
(800) 932-4593 • www.prestwickhouse.com

Table of Contents

INTRODUCTION

*V*ocabulary Power Plus for the New SAT* combines classroom-tested vocabulary drills with reading and writing exercises designed to prepare students for the revised Scholastic Assessment Test; however, *Vocabulary Power Plus for the New SAT* is a resource for all students—not just those who are college bound or preparing for the SAT I. This series is intended to increase vocabulary, improve grammar, enhance writing, and boost critical reading skills for students at all levels of learning.

Critical Reading exercises include lengthy passages and detailed questions. We use SAT-style grammar and writing exercises and have placed the vocabulary words in a non-alphabetical sequence.

To reflect the changes to the Writing and Critical Reading portions of the SAT I, Prestwick House includes inferential exercises instead of the analogical reasoning sections. Coupled with words-in-context activities, inferences cultivate comprehensive word discernment by prompting students to create contexts for words instead of simply memorizing definitions.

The writing exercises in *Vocabulary Power Plus for the New SAT* are process-oriented, but they bring students a step closer to SAT success by exposing them to rubrics that simulate those of the SAT essay-writing component. This exposure to an objective scoring process helps students develop a concrete understanding of writing fundamentals.

We hope that you find the *Vocabulary Power Plus for the New SAT* series to be an effective tool for teaching new words and an exceptional tool for preparing for the new SAT.

Strategies for Completing Activities

Roots, Prefixes, and Suffixes

A knowledge of roots, prefixes, and suffixes can give readers the ability to view unfamiliar words as mere puzzles that require only a few simple steps to solve. For the person interested in the history of words, this knowledge provides the ability to track word origin and evolution. For those who seek to improve vocabulary, this knowledge creates a sure and lifelong method; however, there are two points to remember:

1. Some words have evolved through usage, so present definitions might differ from what you infer through an examination of the roots and prefixes. The word *abstruse*, for example, contains the prefix *ab* (away) and the root *trudere* (to thrust), and literally means *to thrust away*. Today, *abstruse* is used to describe something that is hard to understand.

2. Certain roots do not apply to all words that use the same form. If you know that the root *vin* means "to conquer," then you would be correct in concluding that the word *invincible* means "incapable of being conquered"; however, if you tried to apply the same root meaning to *vindicate* or *vindictive*, you would be incorrect. When analyzing unfamiliar words, check for other possible roots if your inferred meaning does not fit the context.

Despite these considerations, a knowledge of roots and prefixes is one of the best ways to build a powerful vocabulary.

Critical Reading

Reading questions generally fall into several categories.

1. *Identifying the main idea or the author's purpose.* Generally, the question will ask, "What is this selection about?"

In some passages, the author's purpose will be easy to identify because the one or two ideas leap from the text; however, other passages might not be so easily analyzed, especially if they include convoluted sentences. Inverted sentences (subject at the end of the sentence) and elliptical sentences (words missing) will also increase the difficulty of the passages, but all these obstacles can be overcome if readers take one sentence at a time and recast it in their own words. Consider the following sentence:

> These writers either jot down their thoughts bit by bit, in short, ambiguous, and paradoxical sentences, which apparently mean much more than they say—of this kind of writing Schelling's treatises on natural philosophy are a splendid instance; or else they hold forth with a deluge of words and the most intolerable diffusiveness, as though no end of fuss were necessary to make the reader understand the deep meaning of their sentences, whereas it is some quite simple if not actually trivial idea, examples of which may be found in plenty in the popular works of Fichte, and the philosophical manuals of a hundred other miserable dunces.

If we edit out some of the words, the main point of this sentence is obvious.

> These writers either jot down their thoughts bit by bit, in short,
> sentences, which apparently mean much
> more than they say
>
> or   they hold
> a deluge of words
> as
> though   necessary to make the reader understand
> the deep meaning of their sentences

Some sentences need only a few deletions for clarification, but others require major recasting and additions; they must be read carefully and put into the reader's own words.

> Some in their discourse desire rather commendation of wit, in being able to hold all arguments, than of judgment, in discerning what is true; as if it were a praise to know what might be said, and not what should be thought.

After studying it, a reader might recast the sentence as follows:

> In conversation, some people desire praise for their abilities to maintain the conversation rather than their abilities to identify what is true or false, as though it were better to sound good than to know what is truth or fiction.

2. Identifying the stated or implied meaning. *What is the author stating or suggesting?*

The literal meaning of a text does not always correspond with the intended meaning. To understand a passage fully, readers must determine which meaning—if there is more than one—is the intended meaning of the passage.

Consider the following sentence:

> If his notice was sought, an expression of courtesy and interest gleamed out upon his features; proving that there was light within him and that it was only the outward medium of the intellectual lamp that obstructed the rays in their passage.

Interpreted literally, this Nathaniel Hawthorne metaphor suggests that a light-generating lamp exists inside the human body. Since this is impossible, the reader must look to the metaphoric meaning of the passage to understand it properly. In the metaphor, Hawthorne refers to the human mind—consciousness—as a lamp that emits light, and other people cannot always see the lamp because the outside "medium"—the human body—sometimes blocks it.

3. Identifying the tone or mood of the selection. *What feeling does the text evoke?*

To answer these types of questions, readers must look closely at individual words and their connotations; for example, the words *stubborn* and *firm* have almost the same definition, but a writer who describes a character as *stubborn* rather than *firm* is probably suggesting something negative about the character.

Writing

The new SAT allocates only twenty-five minutes to the composition of a well-organized, fully developed essay. Writing a satisfactory essay in this limited time requires facility in determining a thesis, organizing ideas, and producing adequate examples to support the ideas.

An essay written in twenty minutes might not represent the best process in writing—an SAT essay might lack the perfection and depth that weeks of proofreading and editing give to research papers. Process is undoubtedly important, but students must consider the time constraints of the SAT. Completion of the essay is just as important as organization, development, and language use.

The thesis, the organization of ideas, and the support make the framework of a good essay. Before the actual writing begins, writers must create a mental outline by establishing a thesis, or main idea, and one or more specific supporting ideas (the number of ideas will depend on the length and content of the essay). Supporting ideas should not be overcomplicated; they are simply ideas that justify or explain the thesis. The writer must introduce and explain each supporting idea, and the resultant supporting paragraph should answer the *why?* or *who cares?* questions that the thesis may evoke.

Once the thesis and supporting ideas are identified, writers must determine the order in which the ideas will appear in the essay. A good introduction usually explains the thesis and briefly introduces the supporting ideas. Explanation of the supporting ideas should follow, with each idea in its own paragraph. The final paragraph, the conclusion, usually restates the thesis or summarizes the main ideas of the essay.

Adhering to the mental outline when the writing begins will help the writer organize and develop the essay. Using the Organization and Development scoring guides to evaluate practice essays will help to reinforce the process skills. The Word Choice and Sentence Formation scoring guides will help to strengthen language skills—the vital counterpart to essay organization and development.

Pronunciation Guide

a — track
ā — mate
ä — father
â — care
e — pet
ē — be
i — bit
ī — bite
o — job
ō — wrote
ô — port, **fought**
ōō — proof
u — pun
ū — **you**
û — purr
ə — about, system, **supper**, circus
oi — toy

Word List

Lesson 10
affiliate
bane
berate
blatant
calumny
dawdle
desolate
fallible
fawn
filch
garble
minion
neophyte
pacify
prevaricate

Lesson 11
carp
emissary
facade
flagrant
fracas
futile
gait
genesis
immaculate
kindred
lacerate
nefarious
patrician
query
queue

Lesson 12
anthropomorphic
aplomb
beneficiary
careen
catholic
deluge
eerie
fester
guile
havoc
languish
martial
modicum
pall
rancid

Lesson 13
anachronism
defunct
denigrate
effusive
embroil
envisage
gape
haughty
holocaust
humane
impertinent
lackey
lament
lethal
nemesis

Lesson 14
alacrity
benediction
carnage
catalyst
deify
epitaph
foible
frivolous
harp
impel
impetuous
jargon
judicious
lateral
pallid

Lesson 15
adjunct
chicanery
debonair
deplete
equivocal
farcical
feisty
filial
genealogy
gull
impervious
macabre
mitigate
nadir
penchant

Lesson 16
admonish
affliction
aphorism
cache
daub
delete
impermeable
imperturbable
lax
mendicant
obeisance
oscillate
oust
paean
palpable

Lesson 17
aloof
bias
cavort
desecrate
ensue
fiat
fidelity
fluent
gyrate
hilarity
melee
pariah
pedagogue
personification
rambunctious

Lesson 18
allocate
belabor
conjecture
faux
foray
genocide
gratis
manifesto
materialistic
monolithic
predilection
progeny
quintessential
rudimentary
zaftig

Lesson 19
amenable
conducive
influx
junta
mollify
patina
perjury
pinnacle
placebo
plaintive
rigorous
sedentary
stricture
subversive
tantamount

Lesson 20
acumen
concurrent
erroneous
impasse
irrevocable
malodorous
nanotechnology
negligible
notarize
piquant
precept
pungent
renege
visage
wunderkind

Lesson 21
botch
brinkmanship
confute
dynasty
forte
fortitude
ineffable
kleptomania
meritorious
mezzanine
perennial
purport
recumbent
renown
tribulation

Lesson One

1. **licentious** (lī sen´ shəs) *adj.* morally unrestrained
    Like St. Augustine, some people want to abandon their *licentious* lifestyles, but not immediately.
    syn: immoral; lewd   *ant: chaste; pure*

2. **numismatist** (nōō miz´ mə tist) *n.* a coin collector
    My father is a *numismatist* who has hundreds of coins from ancient Rome.

3. **paucity** (pô´ si tē) *n.* a scarcity, lack
    The *paucity* of jobs in the small town forced Jack to find work elsewhere.
    syn: insufficiency   *ant: abundance*

4. **fatalistic** (fāt əl is´ tik) *adj.* believing that all events in life are
    inevitable and determined by fate
    Fatalistic thinkers believe that there is nothing they can do to change the course of their lives.

5. **obtrude** (əb trōōd´) *v.* to force oneself into a situation uninvited
    You were concentrating intently at the work on your desk, so I did not wish to *obtrude*.
    syn: impose; intrude   *ant: extricate*

6. **pensive** (pen´ siv) *adj.* dreamily thoughtful
    Jane was in a *pensive* mood after she finished reading the thought-provoking novel.
    syn: reflective; meditative   *ant: silly; frivolous*

7. **lackadaisical** (lak ə dā´ zi kəl) *adj.* uninterested; listless
    The *lackadaisical* student sat in the detention hall and stared out the window.
    syn: spiritless; apathetic; languid   *ant: enthusiastic; inspired*

8. **alienate** (ā´ lē yə nāt) *v.* to turn away feelings or affections
    Your sarcastic remarks might *alienate* your friends and family.
    syn: estrange; set against   *ant: endear; unite*

9. **elated** (i lā´ tid) *adj.* in high spirits; exultantly proud and joyful
    We were *elated* to learn that our team would move on to finals.
    syn: overjoyed   *ant: depressed*

10. **epigram** (ep´ i gram) *n.* a witty saying expressing a single thought or observation
    The author placed relevant *epigrams* at the beginning of each chapter.
    syn: *aphorism; bon mot; quip*

EXERCISE I—Words in Context

From the list below, supply the words needed to complete the paragraph. Some words will not be used.

alienate	epigram	fatalistic	licentious
obtrude	lackadaisical	paucity	

1. Byron's ___fatalistic___ notion that he possessed no control over his decisions eventually became his excuse for living a[n] ___licentious___ lifestyle. He partied nightly, and his ___paucity___ of ambition or goals had ___alienated___ him from his relatively successful friends. When they tried to talk to Byron about his future, his only response was a[n] ___lackadaisical___ stare.

From the list below, supply the words needed to complete the paragraph. Some words will not be used.

elated	obtrude	alienate	numismatist
pensive	epigram	paucity	

2. Jenny, who lives by Ben Franklin's ___epigram___, "Early to bed and early to rise, makes a man healthy, wealthy, and wise," arrived at the flea market at six a.m. It took her two hours to find what she was looking for—a pre-Revolution Era silver dollar. A[n] ___pensive___ elderly woman sat behind the stand in the shade of a canvas tarp, reading a leather-bound novel.
    "I'm sorry to ___obtrude___," said Jenny, "but what are you asking for this old coin?" The old woman looked up from her book, smiled, and said, "Make me an offer." As an experienced ___numismatist___ Jenny knew the exact value of the coin. She offered half, and Jenny was ___elated___ when the woman accepted her offer.

EXERCISE II—Sentence Completion

Complete the sentence in a way that shows you understand the meaning of the italicized vocabulary word.

1. You might *alienate* your friends if you... *ignore them*

2. A *numismatist* might spend his or her evenings... *collecting coins*

3. If you were not invited to the party, then don't *obtrude* by... *entering*

4. One *epigram* that applies to hard work is...

5. The *lackadaisical* player was cut from the team because... *he is lazy*

6. Someone who suffers a *paucity* of willpower might find it difficult to... *study*

7. It is *fatalistic* to think that you will... *die*

8. Bill was *elated* to learn that... *he was alive*

9. The *licentious* soldier was court-martialed for... *raping*

10. Myra became *pensive* when Cal told her that she... *was beautiful*

EXERCISE III—Roots, Prefixes, and Suffixes

Study the entries and answer the questions that follow.

The prefix *pro* means "before" or "in front."
The roots *fab* and *fess* mean "to speak."
The roots *hab* and *hib* mean "to have" or "to possess."

1. *Using literal translations as guidance, define the following words without using a dictionary.*

   A. inhabit
   B. inhibition
   C. prohibit
   D. affable
   E. confab
   F. fabulist

   [handwritten: inhabit - to live in or dwell]
   [handwritten: inhibition - to restrain]
   [handwritten: prohibit - forbid]
   [handwritten: affable < easy to approach]
   [handwritten: confab - informal conversation]
   [handwritten: fabulist - liar]

2. A[n] ___*habit*___ is a tendency to repeat a particular behavior that you might have, and it is often hard to rid yourself of it. If you have a painting that you want people to see, you might _____ it in an art gallery.

3. At college, a[n] _____ might stand in front of a classroom and speak to students. A short story that often features talking animals and a moral is called a[n] _____.

4. List as many words as you can think of that contain the prefix *pro*.

   [handwritten: pronoun   professional]
   [handwritten: prohibit   propaganda]
   [handwritten: proximity]

EXERCISE IV—Inference

Complete the sentences by inferring information about the italicized word from its context.

1. Wayne always *obtrudes* upon our conversations, so if we want to discuss something privately, we should... *[handwritten: hide]*

2. Two prisoners escaped because the *lackadaisical* guard was... *[handwritten: sleeping]*

3. Japan is an industrial power, but its *paucity* of natural resources forces the nation to... *[handwritten: buy from other countries]*

EXERCISE V—Writing

Here is a writing prompt similar to the one you will find on the writing portion of the SAT.

Plan and write an essay based on the following statement:

> The Victorian poet and critic Matthew Arnold said that literature is "at bottom a criticism of life."

Assignment: Do you agree or disagree with Arnold's view that literature is a criticism of life? Write an essay in which you support or refute Arnold's position. Support your point with evidence from your reading, classroom studies, and experience. Your support should include references to at least one work of literature that you have read.

Thesis: Write a one-sentence response to the assignment. Make certain this single sentence offers a clear statement of your position.

Example: Matthew Arnold is right about literature being a criticism of life because the best literature is that which accurately depicts the good and bad parts of real life.

Organizational Plan: If your thesis is the point on which you want to end, where does your essay need to begin? List the points of development that are inevitable in leading your reader from your beginning point to your end point. This is your outline.

Draft: Use your thesis as both your beginning and your end. Following your outline, write a good first draft of your essay. Remember to support all your points with examples, facts, references to reading, etc.

Review and Revise: Exchange essays with a classmate. Using the scoring guide for Organization on page 221, score your partner's essay (while he or she scores yours). Focus on the organizational plan and use of language conventions. If necessary, rewrite your essay to improve the organizational plan and/or your use of language.

Identifying Sentence Errors

Identify the grammatical error in each of the following sentences. If the sentence contains no error, select answer choice E.

1. <u>Her sister</u> and <u>her</u> are <u>now employed</u> at Beef Barn <u>as cooks</u>.
    (A)   (B)   (C)   (D)
    <u>No error</u>
    (E)

2. <u>While dad slept</u> the <u>toddlers</u> <u>wrote</u> on the walls with <u>crayons</u>.
    (A)   (B)   (C)   (D)
    <u>No error</u>
    (E)

3. <u>An important</u> <u>function</u> of helicopters <u>are</u> <u>search and rescue</u>
    (A)   (B)   (C)   (D)
    capability.   <u>No error</u>
    (E)

4. <u>The mechanic</u> told Bill and <u>I</u> <u>that</u> the car <u>was not finished</u>.
    (A)   (B) (C)   (D)
    <u>No error</u>
    (E)

5. <u>Greg</u> <u>only</u> <u>threw</u> the shot put <u>twenty feet</u>.   <u>No error</u>
    (A)   (B)   (C)   (D)   (E)

Improving Sentences

The underlined portion of each sentence below contains some flaw. Select the answer choice that best corrects the flaw.

6.   Last night, <u>I slept like a log</u>.
    A. I slept like a baby.
    B. I slept well.
    C. I slept as if there were no tomorrow.
    D. I did not sleep at all.
    E. I slept like my dog.

7.   Going to school is <u>preferable than</u> going to work.
    A. not preferable than
    B. preferable
    C. perforated to
    D. preferable to
    E. preferable than

8.   <u>Wild and vicious, the veterinarian examined the wounded panther</u>.
    A. The wild and vicious wounded panther was examined by the veterinarian.
    B. The veterinarian examined the wounded, wild, and vicious panther.
    C. The wild and vicious veterinarian examined the wounded panther.
    D. Wild and vicious, the examined panther wounded the veterinarian.
    E. Wild and vicious, the veterinarian examined the wounded panther.

9.   <u>Journalists are</u> stimulated by his or her deadline.
    A. A journalist are
    B. Journalism is
    C. Journalists is
    D. A journalist is
    E. Journalists are

10.   When <u>someone has</u> been drinking, they are more likely to speed.
    A. someone has
    B. a person has
    C. a driver has
    D. someone have
    E. drivers have

Lesson Two

1. **amalgamate** (ə mal´ gə māt) *v.* to combine
    The great leader *amalgamated* many small tribes into his own to make a singular, powerful nation.
    syn: unite; blend; merge; consolidate   *ant: splinter; disunite*

2. **demented** (di men´ tid) *adj.* mentally ill; insane
    Mary's *demented* cat attacks anything that makes a noise, including the television.
    syn: deranged; insane   *ant: sane*

3. **hone** (hōn) *v.* to sharpen
    The butcher used a whetstone to *hone* his knives until they were razor sharp.
                         ant: dull

4. **beleaguer** (bi lē´ gər) *v.* to besiege by encircling (as with an army); to harass
    The mosquitoes will *beleaguer* you if you venture near the swamp.
    syn: surround; annoy   *ant: evade*

5. **gorge** (gôrj) *v.* to eat or swallow greedily
    The beagle *gorged* itself after it chewed through the bag of dog food.

6. **antiquated** (an´ ti kwā tid) *adj.* no longer used or useful; very old
    The *antiquated* washboard hung on the wall, useful only as a decoration.
    syn: obsolete; out-of-date; archaic   *ant: modern*

7. **opiate** (ō´ pē it) *n.* a narcotic used to cause sleep or bring relief from pain
    The veterinarian used an *opiate* to sedate the wounded animal.
                         ant: stimulant

8. **caricature** (kar´ i kə chûr) *n.* an exaggerated portrayal of one's features
    The *caricature* of the mayor in the political cartoon exaggerated the size of his ears and nose.
    syn: mockery; cartoon

9. **dally** (dal´ ē) *v.* to waste time; to dawdle
    If you *dally* too long in making a decision, someone else will buy the car you want.
    syn: dawdle; loiter   *ant: hasten; hurry*

10. **felonious** (fə lō´ nē əs) *adj.* pertaining to or constituting a major crime
The inmate expected to be released from prison early, despite the many *felonious* activities on his record.
syn: criminal

EXERCISE I—Words in Context

From the list below, supply the words needed to complete the paragraph. Some words will not be used.

antiquated	gorge	caricature	felonious
opiate	dally	beleaguer	

1. Alex crouched behind a palm tree and shook her head; she had escaped from her cell, but she was still woozy from the _____ that her captors used to drug her. She didn't _____, because the guards would be searching for her in a matter of minutes. Knowing that it might be days before she would eat again, Alex _____ herself on a bag lunch that one of the guards had left unattended near her cell. Seconds later, she began looking for the _____ truck that the guards had used to transport her to the compound. She knew that the outmoded vehicle wouldn't set any speed records, but it was her only option for getting back to civilization. The odds were against Alex, but she had to make it out of the jungle before she could expose the kingpin's _____ operation to the public.

From the list below, supply the words needed to complete the paragraph. Some words will not be used.

dally	caricature	beleaguer	hone
amalgamate	felonious	demented	

2. Doctor Rearick, a famous chemist, mused at the _____ of himself in the editorial cartoon. The artist had depicted the aging chemist as a[n] _____ scientist, like Victor Frankenstein or Doctor Moreau, at a lab table trying to _____ two mysterious liquids by pouring them both into a steaming test tube. Reporters _____ him with phone calls for days after he announced the discovery of a remarkable new alloy, and Rearick knew that he would need to _____ his public speaking skills before he explained the full significance of the discovery in front of the television news cameras.

EXERCISE II—Sentence Completion

Complete the sentence in a way that shows you understand the meaning of the italicized vocabulary word.

1. The doctor administered an *opiate* to the patient to...

2. If you *dally* in finishing your report, you might...

3. People think that she's *demented* just because she...

4. The political cartoonist's *caricature* depicted the president as...

5. The seagulls *beleaguered* the people on the beach until...

6. You should first *hone* your skills if you plan to...

7. The teacher told us not to *amalgamate* those chemicals because...

8. Bert *gorged* himself at the buffet because he...

9. Andy's *felonious* behavior finally caught up to him when...

10. Paul replaced his *antiquated* computer because it...

EXERCISE III—Roots, Prefixes, and Suffixes

Study the entries and answer the questions that follow.

The prefix *sub* means "under" or "below."
The suffix *ize* means "to make."
The root *urb* means "city."

1. Using literal translations as guidance, define the following words without using a dictionary.

    A. suburb   D. standardize
    B. urbanize   E. subhuman
    C. substandard   F. humanize

2. A[n] _____ is a vessel that travels underwater, and a *subway* train travels _____ the ground.

3. List as many words as you can think of that contain the prefix *sub* or the suffix *ize*.

EXERCISE IV—Inference

Complete the sentences by inferring information about the italicized word from its context.

1. If Kevin needs a large bowl to *amalgamate* the ingredients, he is probably going to...

2. If an angry mob *beleaguered* the driver of the car, then the driver was probably...

3. Nolan went to the library to *hone* his understanding of chemistry by...

EXERCISE V—Critical Reading

Below is a reading passage followed by several multiple-choice questions similar to the ones you will encounter on the SAT. Carefully read the passage and choose the best answer to each of the questions.

The author of the following passage explains recent astronomical discoveries and their significance to humanity.

1   Humans have fantasized about the significance of planets ever since the ancients first identified the "wandering stars." Planets are fundamental to mythology and astrology, and as we indulge our imaginations with the future of humanity, planets are essential to our visions of interstellar endeavors, both in fiction and in fact. Recent discoveries have revealed plenty of new material for our imaginations. Our civilization may lack the technology to set foot on the eight unexplored planets of our own solar system, but that can't prevent us from compiling a list of new planets to explore when we finally do have the technology.

2   In 1991, Alexander Wolszczan, an astronomy professor from Penn State University, used a radio telescope to time signals that revealed three planets orbiting a very distant pulsar. Located more than 1000 light years from Earth in the constellation Virgo, two of the planets resemble Earth in density while the third is moon-sized. The probability of life on the planets is low; due to their proximity to the pulsar, the planets endure a constant bombardment of radiation that would render them inhospitable. The planets are probably barren, lifeless worlds, but such speculation is only secondary to the paramount discovery: planets exist elsewhere in the galaxy. Their simple existence is enough to confirm that our own solar system is only one of possible billions elsewhere in the galaxy—and we have the means to detect them.

3   The next major extrasolar planet discovery occurred in 1995, when Michel Mayor and Didier Queloz used spectrographic data to discover a large planet orbiting 51 Pegasi, a star that resembles our own sun. The planet is likely a gas giant similar to our own Jupiter, but its correlation with a sun-like star inspires high hopes that a solar system like our own will eventually be found.

4   Since 1995, astronomers have added more than 115 new planets to their list of discoveries, some of which exist in multiple-planet systems. Most of the discovered planets are Jovian, as that of the 51 Pegasi system, but that, astronomers stress, is due to our limited detection methods.

5   Extrasolar planets are invisible to optical telescopes. Researchers instead rely upon the behavior of parent stars to signal the presence of planets. As any planet orbits a star, the two bodies pull themselves toward each other due to gravity. For an observer who has a side view of the celestial process, the parent star will appear to "wobble." All stars with planets exhibit this behavior, but large planets that orbit close to their parent stars cause enough wobble that we can detect it from hundreds of light years away. By identifying and measuring the wobble of the parent stars, astronomers confirm the presence of planets and calculate planetary mass.

6   Discoveries become increasingly noteworthy as astronomers refine extrasolar detection techniques. At the time in which the first pulsar planets were discovered, researchers found mainly gas giants in close proximity to the parent stars. Researchers are now discovering planetary systems that contain increasingly smaller planets with longer orbits. The significance? As we discover planetary systems with smaller planets further from their parent stars, we approach the day in which we find the smallest of planets: terrestrial planets, like Earth. Where terrestrial planets exist, conditions for known forms of life could exist. The discovery of extraterrestrial life could reroute the collective attention, philosophies, and endeavors of our civilization.

7   Even if we are unable to find any terrestrial planets, astronomers theorize that our next major extrasolar discovery might be that of planetary satellites. If the Jovian planets that have been discovered are anything like Jupiter and Saturn, then there is a probability that they will have satellites—Jupiter has thirty-nine known satellites, and Saturn has at least eighteen. Some of the satellites in our solar system, such as Saturn's Titan and Jupiter's Io, have atmospheres. The satellite atmospheres in our solar system might be inhospitable to life, but what about the satellites of the newly discovered giants?

8   Is it possible that a satellite of one of the newly discovered planets, 100 parsecs away, could have atmospheric conditions like those of our nurturing Earth? Time and technology will tell, but at least we now know, thanks to early extrasolar explorers, where to direct our attention in the human quest for answers.

1.   The primary purpose of this passage is to
      A. offer theories on the formation of planets.
      B. explain how new planets are detected.
      C. discuss the impact of new discoveries.
      D. dispute heliocentric theory.
      E. inform readers about the discovery of new planets.

2.   The overall tone of this passage is
      A. descriptive.
      B. humorous.
      C. speculative.
      D. optimistic.
      E. simplistic.

3.   Which of the following would be the best substitute for *proximity* in paragraph 2?
      A. size
      B. aloofness
      C. remoteness
      D. gravitational pull
      E. nearness

4. According to paragraph 2, why are the pulsar planets probably devoid of life?
   A. The pulsar bombards the planets with radiation.
   B. The pulsar creates extreme temperatures on the planets.
   C. The planets lack atmospheres.
   D. Life has been detected on the planets.
   E. The planets rotate too quickly.

5. As used in paragraph 4, the word *Jovian* most nearly means
   A. happy.
   B. mythological.
   C. resembling Jupiter.
   D. nonexistent.
   E. small.

6. According to paragraph 5, astronomers discover mostly large planets because
   A. Earth has no telescopes beyond the atmosphere.
   B. small planets do not cause enough wobble to detect from Earth.
   C. small planets burn up while orbiting the parent stars.
   D. the atmospheres of small planets obscure the images.
   E. NASA provides no funding for the research.

7. In paragraph 7, the author lists the known numbers of satellites for Jupiter and Saturn because
   A. it increases the likelihood that the new planets will have satellites.
   B. it impresses the audience with statistics.
   C. it describes how Jupiter and Saturn are unlike the discovered planets.
   D. it provides an example that supports the new planets having satellites.
   E. it emphasizes the argument for space exploration.

8. Which of the following best describes this passage?
   A. specific and explanatory
   B. conjectural and cynical
   C. abridged and speculative
   D. thorough and comprehensive
   E. researched and scholarly

9.   What would make the best title for this passage?
     A.   Techniques of Planetary Detection
     B.   Planets in Virgo
     C.   The Search for Life
     D.   The Space Frontier: Specks on the Horizon
     E.   Astronomers Find Planets

10. This passage would most likely be found in a/an
     A.   encyclopedia.
     B.   fiction novel.
     C.   history book.
     D.   book about new astronomy techniques.
     E.   exploration magazine.

Lesson Three

1. **edifice** (ed´ ə fis) *n.* a large, elaborate structure; an imposing building
The palace was not just a home; it was an *edifice* that created envy among foreign rulers.
syn: fortress   *ant: hovel*

2. **ambidextrous** (am bi dek´ strəs) *adj.* equally skillful with either hand
The *ambidextrous* woman could write both left- and right-handed.

3. **belated** (bi lā´ tid) *adj.* delayed
Joan sent a *belated* birthday card to her sister.
syn: tardy; late   *ant: timely*

4. **animate** (an´ ə māt) *v.* to give life or motion to
A trip to the ice cream parlor helped to *animate* the sullen child.
syn: enliven; encourage; excite   *ant: quell*

5. **knead** (nēd) *v.* to work dough or clay into a uniform mixture
It is easier to *knead* dough with an electric mixer than by hand.
syn: squeeze; rub; press

6. **chauvinist** (shō´ və nist) *n.* one having a fanatical devotion to a country, gender, or religion, with contempt for other countries, the opposite sex, or other beliefs
He did not dislike women, but he was a *chauvinist* when it came to hiring women for management positions.

7. **egalitarian** (i gal i ter´ ē ən) *adj.* promoting equal rights for all people
The equal rights amendment for women was founded on *egalitarian* principles.
         ant: elitist

8. **berserk** (bər sûrk´) *adj.* in a state of violent or destructive rage
My father almost went *berserk* when I told him I had dented his new car.
syn: frenzied   *ant: placid; complacent*

9. **ostentatious** (os ten tā´ shəs) *adj.* marked by a conspicuous, showy, or pretentious display
The *ostentatious* charity ball cost the guests $2,000 per plate.
syn: grandiose   *ant: unobtrusive; bland*

10. **delude** (di lōōd´) v. to mislead; to fool
The fast-talking salesman could not *delude* us into buying the dilapidated truck.
syn: deceive   *ant: enlighten*

EXERCISE I—Words in Context

From the list below, supply the words needed to complete the paragraph. Some words will not be used.

delude   edifice   berserk   ostentatious   animate

1. The old Lane estate was a[n] _____ that towered over the other homes in the neighborhood. It had a[n] _____ courtyard more suitable for a palace, and rows of shimmering Aspen trees seemed to _____ the grounds when they fluttered with even the mildest breeze. The elaborate exterior of the mansion might _____ someone into thinking that the house must be beautiful inside, but actually, the roof leaks, the paint is peeling, and the floors creak.

From the list below, supply the words needed to complete the paragraph. Some words will not be used.

chauvinist   ostentatious   belated   egalitarian

2. The corporation claimed to endorse _____ company policies, but some of the managers were _____ who refused to promote anyone not native to Scandinavia. One of the foreign employees eventually filed suit against the company, and in two years was awarded the _____ promotion he had long deserved.

From the list below, supply the words needed to complete the paragraph. Some words will not be used.

ambidextrous   berserk   knead   edifice

3. Laurie _____ the modeling clay until it was soft enough to work with. Since her work required deep concentration, she nearly went _____ when her assistant interrupted for the third time to obtain Laurie's signature. Even though Laurie was _____, she could not sign her name and focus on her art simultaneously.

EXERCISE II—Sentence Completion

Complete the sentence in a way that shows you understand the meaning of the italicized vocabulary word.

1. Janet bought a *belated* graduation gift for Mike because she...

2. The *ambidextrous* pitcher could throw...

3. In an *egalitarian* nation, everyone has the...

4. One *edifice* that most people have seen in pictures is...

5. The soccer player *kneaded* her calf muscle because...

6. Though he was quite wealthy, the miser's home lacked *ostentatious* art-work or furniture because he...

7. The sound of food pouring into a metal dish *animated*...

8. Uncle Phil was admittedly a male *chauvinist* who believed that...

9. Don't let the resort's brochure *delude* you; we went there last year, and the pictures in the guide are...

10. Rabies caused the dog to act *berserk*, so...

EXERCISE III—Roots, Prefixes, and Suffixes

Study the entries and answer the questions that follow.

The roots *mater* and *matr* mean "mother."
The root *micro* means "small."
The root *meter* means "measure."
The root *aut* means "self."

1. Using literal translations as guidance, define the following words without using a dictionary.

    A. alma mater   D. microprocessor
    B. matron   E. micrometer
    C. matrimony   F. automatic

2. Mothers are known to have certain _____ instincts, especially with regard to caring for their children. In a *matriarchal* society, family lineage is traced through the _____'s side of the family instead of the father's side.

3. If *cosmos* means "world," then a *microcosm* must be _____.
    Microbes are so _____ that you need a[n] _____ to see them.

4. List as many words as you can think of that contain the roots *meter* or *auto*.

EXERCISE IV—Inference

Complete the sentences by inferring information about the italicized word from its context.

1. If the mad doctor wants to try to *animate* the lifeless monster, then he or she wants to...

2. An *ambidextrous* golfer would not need to worry about having left- or right-handed clubs because...

3. If Karen was angry that Mark did not follow through with his *egalitarian* plan, then Mark must have...

EXERCISE V—Writing

Here is a writing prompt similar to the one you will find on the writing portion of the SAT.

Plan and write an essay based on the following statement:

The happiest day in all my outer life!

> For in an old shed full of tools and lumber at the end of the garden, and half-way between an empty fowl-house and a disused stable (each an Eden in itself) I found a small toy-wheelbarrow—quite the most extraordinary, the most unheard of and undreamed of, humorously, daintily, exquisitely fascinating object I had ever come across in all my brief existence.
>
> –George du Maurier (1834-1896), *Peter Ibbetson*

Assignment: Your opinion of what was extraordinary during your youth might be quite different from that of George du Maurier's wheelbarrow. In an essay, explain something that was "unheard of, undreamed of" or "exquisitely fascinating" when you were a child. Explain where you found it, and what it meant to you. Compare this object to things that you hold as important today, and explain their significance in your life. Support your idea with evidence from your reading, classroom studies, experience, and observation.

Thesis: Write a one-sentence response to the assignment. Make certain this single sentence offers a clear statement of your position.

Example: The object of fascination during my youth, which still captivates me today, is a secluded cave deep in the forest, that I discovered while on a camping trip.

Development of Ideas: If your thesis is the point on which you want to end, what facts or examples can you offer your readers to help them see your point? Make a thorough list of specific facts and examples. Number them in the order in which you think they should best be discussed. This list is your outline.

Draft: Use your thesis as both your beginning and your end. Following your outline, write a good first draft of your essay. Remember to support all of your points with examples, facts, references to reading, etc.

Review and Revise: Exchange essays with a classmate. Using the scoring guide for Development of Ideas on page 222, score your partner's essay (while he or she scores yours). Focus on the development of ideas and use of language conventions. If necessary, rewrite your essay to incorporate more (or more relevant) support and/or to improve your use of language.

Improving Paragraphs

Read the following passage and then answer the multiple-choice questions that follow. The questions will require you to make decisions regarding the revision of the reading selection.

(1) The most beautiful women occasionally look plain. (2) The plainest women have a few beautiful moments in their lives. (3) Beauty is such an intangible thing that it would puzzle the wisest men to define it.

(4) No one need despair. (5) We will try together to find out some of the subtle secrets of beauty; and who can tell what unlovely little buds may open out into lovely flowers by discovering some of those points of attractiveness which every woman possesses, though some from shyness or from faults of education, shut them away and hide them as though they were crimes.

(6) We have seen beautiful faces without a good feature, we have seen perfectly regular features unaccompanied by that wonderful presence. (7) Some faces are beautiful in repose and positively ugly in movement. (8) Abundant hair and expressive eyes sometimes are enough. (9) Others, plain in feature, brighten into real loveliness in speech, smiles or laughter.

(10) A lovely mouth and dimpled chin often redeem an otherwise plain face. (11) Every novel we take up has a more or less attractive heroine, but in how few cases does the author convey to the mind the idea of any special loveliness. (12) As Byron says, it is impossible to describe beauty, and it is quite as impossible to be sure of its presence or absence.

(13) While we are looking at a lovely face, wondering at its loveliness, a cloud of thought, or perhaps temper crosses it, and the beauty is gone; or we may be thinking, while looking on some plain face, "How hopelessly unattractive!" when suddenly some wave of emotion lights up the eyes, alters the lines, softens the curves, warms the coloring, and there before us is beauty, visible and unmistakable.

–From the *Sunlight Almanac*, 1896

1. Which revision of sentence 3 best introduces the main idea of the passage?
   A. Beauty cannot be defined by even the wisest people, unless they realize that beauty is nothing more than an intangible emotion.
   B. Beauty, being intangible, is in the eye of the beholder.
   C. Beauty is such an intangible thing that it would puzzle the wisest men to define it; however, they would agree that beauty depends not so much on one's natural features as how those features are presented.
   D. No one can define beauty because it is a balance of two things.
   E. While beauty is intangible and difficult to define, natural features will always be the basis for measuring one's degree of beauty; however, the wisest men are puzzled by beauty's being a blend of looks and motion.

2. The readability of paragraph 2 is impaired by which error?
   A. Sentence 5 is a run-on with complicated modifiers.
   B. Sentence 4 is unnecessary and should be deleted.
   C. The "subtle secrets" should be explained.
   D. Sentence 4 should be combined with sentence 5.
   E. Sentence 5 should precede sentence 4.

3. Which of the following corrects a grammatical error in paragraph 3?
   A. Insert a dash after *smiles*.
   B. Insert *and* after the comma in sentence 6.
   C. Replace *presence* with *presents*.
   D. Insert a semicolon after *repose*.
   E. Exchange *sometimes* and *enough*.

4. The best way to improve the development of paragraph 4 is to
   A. move sentence 10 to the end of paragraph 4.
   B. move sentence 10 to the end of paragraph 3.
   C. combine paragraphs 4 and 5.
   D. move sentence 11 to the end of paragraph 4.
   E. move sentence 10 to paragraph 5.

5. The passage is most suitable for use as
   A. an introduction to a lesson on poise.
   B. an article on the history of hairstyles.
   C. instructions for applying makeup.
   D. an article about nineteenth-century culture.
   E. an argument that beauty does not exist.

Lesson Four

1. **elude** (i lo͞od´) *v.* to escape notice; to get away from
   The prisoner tried to *elude* the guards by hiding in the laundry truck.
   syn: avoid; evade; lose   *ant: attract*

2. **fallow** (fal´ō) *adj.* inactive; unproductive
   A *fallow* mind needs to be stimulated with challenging ideas and projects.
   syn: idle; barren   *ant: fertile; productive*

3. **blight** (blīt) *n.* anything that destroys, prevents growth, or causes devaluation
   The junkyard was a *blight* on the otherwise appealing neighborhood.
   syn: affliction; disease   *ant: enhancement*

4. **obsequy** (ob´sə kwē) *n.* a funeral rite or ceremony
   The explorers held brief *obsequies* for their fallen leader before burying him on the side of the mountain.

5. **denizen** (den´i zən) *n.* an occupant; inhabitant
   Prairie dogs are *denizens* of the Great Plains, so it is unlikely that you would see one in Maine.
   syn: resident   *ant: emigrant; alien*

6. **fealty** (fē´əl tē) *n.* obligated loyalty or faithfulness
   Peasants who did not show any *fealty* to the duke often disappeared.
   syn: devotion; fidelity; allegiance   *ant: disloyalty; treachery*

7. **entice** (en tīs´) *v.* to attract by offering reward or pleasure
   The styling and color of the gown *enticed* me, but I could not afford such an extravagant purchase.
   syn: tempt; lure   *ant: discourage*

8. **gratify** (grat´ə fī) *v.* to please
   To *gratify* the pouting child, his mother handed him a lollipop.
   syn: satisfy; indulge   *ant: displease; disappoint*

9. **laggard** (lag´ərd) *n.* a slow person, especially one who falls behind
   Wear good shoes on the hike, or you'll be a *laggard* and delay the entire group.
   syn: straggler; dawdler   *ant: leader*

10. **gambit** (gam´ bit) *n.* maneuver or action used to gain an advantage
    The general's *gambit* sacrificed many soldiers, but ultimately won the battle.
    syn: strategy; ploy; maneuver   *ant: blunder*

EXERCISE I—Words in Context

From the list below, supply the words needed to complete the paragraph. Some words will not be used.

fealty	entice	elude	fallow
blight	denizen	gambit	

1. Overuse of the soil and an extended drought contributed to the _____ known in history as the Dust Bowl. In the Midwest, _____ fields lay barren for a decade, forcing many _____ of the community to give up their farms and seek employment in the cities, where industry _____ them with promises of steady, but ultimately minuscule, paychecks. In the years that followed the Dust Bowl, farmers stopped over-plowing fields because they knew that no one could _____ nature's wrath.

From the list below, supply the words needed to complete the paragraph. Some words will not be used.

laggard	entice	gambit	obsequy
denizen	fealty	gratify	

2. The king knew that his plan for a surprise attack would be a[n] _____ that would test the _____ of his soldiers, but it was the only chance he had of thwarting the invading fleet. Speed would be the key to success; one _____ in the ranks could jeopardize the entire operation if the soldier were not in place at the right time. As an incentive to fight well, the king promised to _____ each soldier with twenty acres of land after the battle. The promise was unprecedented, but on the other hand, if the army should fail, then the soldiers would be lucky to have proper _____ because the invaders did not plan to take prisoners.

EXERCISE II—Sentence Completion

Complete the sentence in a way that shows you understand the meaning of the italicized vocabulary word.

1.   The manager *gratified* the complaining customer by…

2.   The oil spill was a *blight* that caused…

3.   The villagers had limited *fealty* for the new king because he…

4.   Tim tried to *elude* the mosquitoes by…

5.   Mikhail's *gambit* during the chess game cost him…

6.   Many *denizens* of the beach community like to…

7.   The *laggard* didn't get tickets to the concert because he…

8.   The brochure *enticed* Annette to visit the island because…

9.   The *fallow* economy forced many investors to…

10.   Instead of a typical *obsequy*, the dying man requested…

EXERCISE III—Roots, Prefixes, and Suffixes

Study the entries and answer the questions that follow.

The root *chroma* means "color."
The prefix *mono* means "one."
The prefix *poly* means "many."
The root *morph* means "form" or "shape."

1. Using literal translations as guidance, define the following words without using a dictionary.

    A. polychromatic   D. polymorphic
    B. monochromatic   E. monorail
    C. polygon   F. monosyllabic

2. Someone who speaks in a single pitch, whose voice does not raise or lower, is said to speak in a[n] _____. Doing _____ thing might become *monotonous* after a few hours.

3. List as many words as you can think of that contain the prefix *poly* or the root *morph*.

EXERCISE IV—Inference

Complete the sentences by inferring information about the italicized word from its context.

1. The team would have won the relay race if it had not been for the *laggard* who...

2. The coach's *gambit* left his players vulnerable, but the bold move...

3. If Lonnie tried to *elude* his friends in the mall, then he probably...

EXERCISE V—Critical Reading

Below is a pair of reading passages followed by several multiple-choice questions similar to the ones you will encounter on the SAT. Carefully read both passages and choose the best answer to each of the questions.

The following passages are two famous military speeches intended to motivate soldiers fighting over the same piece of land: northern Italy. Hannibal, the renowned Carthaginian general, delivered the first speech shortly after the Carthaginian Army astonished the Romans by crossing the Alps. The second passage includes two speeches from Napoleon Bonaparte. In the first part of the passage, Napoleon addresses his troops as they prepare to enter Italy. In the second part, Napoleon's troops are about to take the city of Milan.

Passage 1

Hannibal's Speech to his Soldiers (218 B.C.)

If, soldiers, you shall by and by, in judging of your own fortune, preserve the same feelings which you experienced a little before in the example of the fate of the others, we have already conquered; for neither was that merely a spectacle, but, as it were, a certain representation of your condition. And I know not
5   whether fortune has not thrown around you still stronger chains and more urgent necessities than around your captives. On the right and left two seas enclose you, without your possessing even a single ship for escape. The river Po around you, the Po larger and more impetuous than the Rhone; the Alps behind, scarcely passed by you when fresh and vigorous, hem you in.

10   Here, soldiers, where you have first met the enemy, you must conquer or die; and the same fortune which has imposed the necessity of fighting holds out to you, if victorious, rewards than which men are not wont to desire greater, even from the immortal gods. If we were only about to recover by our valor Sicily and Sardinia, wrested from our fathers, the recompense would be sufficiently ample;
15   but whatever, acquired and amassed by so many triumphs, the Romans possess, all with its masters themselves, will become yours. To gain this rich reward, hasten, then, and seize your arms, with the favor of the gods....

That most cruel and haughty nation considers everything its own, and at its own disposal; it thinks it right that it should regulate with whom we are to have war,
20   with whom peace; it circumscribes and shuts us up by the boundaries of mountains and rivers which we must not pass, and then does not adhere to those boundaries which it appointed....They have sent the two consuls of this year, one to Africa, the other to Spain: there is nothing left to us in any quarter, except what we can assert to ourselves by arms. Those may be cowards and dastards
25   who have something to look back upon; whom, flying through safe and unmolested roads, their own lands and their own country will receive: there is a

necessity for you to be brave, and, since all between victory and death is broken off from you by inevitable despair, either to conquer, or if fortune should waver, to meet death rather in battle than in flight. If this be well fixed and determined
30. in the minds of you all, I will repeat, you have already conquered; no stronger incentive to victory has been given to man by the immortal gods.

Passage 2

Napoleon's Speech to his Soldiers: At the Beginning of the Italian Campaign

Soldiers: You are naked and ill-fed! Government owes you much and can give you nothing. The patience and courage you have shown in the midst of this
5   rocky wilderness are admirable; but they gain you no renown; no glory results to you from your endurance. It is my design to lead you into the most fertile plains of the world. Rich provinces and great cities will be in your power; there you will find honor, glory, and wealth. Soldiers of Italy, will you be wanting in courage or perseverance?

10   Napoleon's Speech to his Soldiers: On Entering Milan

Soldiers: You have rushed like a torrent from the top of the Apennines; you have overthrown and scattered all that opposed your march. Piedmont, delivered from Austrian tyranny, indulges her natural sentiments of peace and friendship toward France. Milan is yours, and the republican flag waves throughout Lombardy. The
15   dukes of Parma and Modena owe their political existence to your generosity alone.

The army which so proudly threatened you can find no barrier to protect it against your courage; neither the Po, the Ticino, nor the Adda could stop you for a single day. These vaunted bulwarks of Italy opposed you in vain; you passed
20   them as rapidly as the Apennines.

These great successes have filled the heart of your country with joy. Your representatives have ordered a festival to commemorate your victories, which has been held in every district of the republic. There your fathers, your mothers, your wives, sisters, and mistresses rejoiced in your good fortune and proudly boasted
25   of belonging to you.

Yes, soldiers, you have done much—but remains there nothing more to do? Shall it be said of us that we knew how to conquer, but not how to make use of victory? Shall posterity reproach us with having found Capua in Lombardy?

But I see you already hasten to arms. An effeminate repose is tedious to you; the
30   days which are lost to glory are lost to your happiness. Well, then, let us set forth!

1. Which choice best describes the intent of lines 5–9 in passage 1?
   A. to remind the soldiers of their own personal strength
   B. to express the difficulty of crossing the Po River
   C. to warn the soldiers about the Roman Navy
   D. to emphasize that the soldiers cannot turn back
   E. to contrast the Po and Rhone Rivers

2. As used in line 14 of the first passage, *recompense* most nearly means
   A. restitution.
   B. sacrifice.
   C. expenditure.
   D. revenge.
   E. satisfaction.

3. According to paragraph 3 of the first passage, why do the Romans deserve to be attacked?
   A. Rome invaded Egypt and Portugal.
   B. The Romans are "cowards and dastards" who deserve war.
   C. The Romans took Sicily and Pisa from Carthage.
   D. Rome is tyrannical and exploitative to the Carthaginians.
   E. The Carthaginians are freezing in the Alps because the Romans have leveled all the forests around them.

4. According to paragraph 1 of the second passage, what should motivate Napoleon's soldiers in battle?
   A. the chance to win more territory for their government
   B. the possibility to demonstrate perseverance in the face of difficulty
   C. the prospect of individual renown and prosperity
   D. the timeless virtues of delayed gratification and bravery
   E. the opportunity to grow successful crops in Italy

5. Napoleon probably uses the simile in line 11 of second passage to
   A. highlight the difficulties the soldiers have faced so far.
   B. emphasize the deliberate pace of the expedition.
   C. express the speed and power of the French invasion.
   D. relieve the soldiers' worries about invading Milan.
   E. downplay the seriousness of previous casualties.

6. As used in line 19 of the second passage, *bulwarks* most nearly means
   A. rivers.
   B. landmarks.
   C. sights.
   D. hallmarks.
   E. obstructions.

7. The tone of the first passage can best be described as
   A. didactic.
   B. restrained.
   C. effusive.
   D. cynical.
   E. sentimental.

8. The authors of both passages have different perspectives of fate. Which of the following identifies the difference?
   A. Only Hannibal downplays the role of government in the future of the war.
   B. Only Napoleon asks the soldiers to be courageous in the face of adversity.
   C. Only Hannibal acknowledges divine intervention as a factor in the war.
   D. Only Napoleon's soldiers are motivated by personal glory and wealth.
   E. Only Napoleon points out the difficulties of the battle ahead.

9. Which of the following identifies a similarity in setting between the two passages?
   A. The generals are addressing their soldiers in the same war.
   B. Both armies are preparing to invade northern Italy.
   C. Both Napoleon and Hannibal appeal to God for intervention.
   D. Both generals point out the shortcomings of their respective governments.
   E. Both generals warn their soldiers about complacency in battle.

10. Which of the following is a motivational factor for the Carthaginians but not for Napoleon's soldiers?
    A. The Carthaginian government has no way to compensate its soldiers.
    B. The Carthaginians are fighting to regain their sovereignty.
    C. The Carthaginians are better at surviving in the wilderness.
    D. The Carthaginians must cross the treacherous Po River.
    E. The Carthaginians fight to conquer; the French fight out of necessity.

Lesson Five

1. **jaded** (jā´ did) *adj.* worn out; dulled, as from overindulgence
   Kate became *jaded* about love after the third boyfriend in a month broke up with her.
   syn: exhausted; wearied   *ant: fresh*

2. **gist** (jist) *n.* the main point
   I never did understand the *gist* of his story.
   syn: idea; essence

3. **advocate** (ad´ və kāt) *v.* to recommend; to speak in favor of
   The neutral organization does not *advocate* support of a particular candidate or position.
   syn: promote; encourage   *ant: oppose; contest*

4. **efface** (i fās´) *v.* to obliterate; to wipe out
   He tried to *efface* his memories of her by burning all her pictures.
   syn: erase   *ant: enshrine*

5. **charisma** (kə riz´ mə) *n.* personal appeal or attraction; magnetism
   The candidate had *charisma* and good looks, but little knowledge of important issues.
   syn: charm

6. **ogre** (ō´ gər) *n.* a brute; a large monster; a frightful giant
   The *ogre* occasionally emerged from his mountain cave and terrorized the villagers.

7. **mesmerize** (mez´ mə rīz) *v.* to hypnotize
   The fast music and spinning dancers *mesmerized* the audience.
   syn: captivate; entrance   *ant: bore*

8. **entity** (en´ ti tē) *n.* anything having existence, either physical or mystical
   Ann thought that she saw a ghostly *entity* hovering over the graveyard, but it turned out to be a flag.

9. **bandy** (ban´ dē) *v.* to exchange words; to discuss casually
   Let's not *bandy* words about the deal any more; just sign the papers and leave, please.

10. **dastardly** (das´ tərd lē) *adj.* cowardly and treacherous
The *dastardly* thief stole money only from helpless, elderly people.
syn: dishonorable; shameful   *ant: righteous*

EXERCISE I—Words in Context

From the list below, supply the words needed to complete the paragraph. Some words will not be used.

charisma	efface	ogre	advocate
gist	bandy	mesmerize	

1. Joan, who _____ the cleanup of the James River, is always trying to gain supporters for her cause. The usual _____ of her speech focuses on the effects of the river's pollution on future generations. Her eloquent speech _____ audiences, and her _____ helps her to win the hearts of people who are not even affected by the James River. Joan hopes someday to _____ the irresponsible dumping practices that continue to foul the James River.

From the list below, supply the words needed to complete the paragraph. Some words will not be used.

dastardly	gist	entity	jaded
ogre	bandy	charisma	

2. The _____ athlete, accustomed to winning first place, wanted to be happy with her third-place trophy, but deep down, she felt that months of intensive training had gone to waste. On the bus ride home, she refused to _____ compliments or even joke about the race with her teammates. She could think only about the _____ runner who intentionally tripped her early in the race and likely cost her the win. Myra could not believe that such an unsportsmanlike _____ was allowed to compete in track meets. Myra didn't see the other girl after the race, but merely thinking of that horrid _____ would haunt Myra for weeks to come.

EXERCISE II—Sentence Completion

Complete the sentence in a way that shows you understand the meaning of the italicized vocabulary word.

1. Sally described enough of the movie for Bill to get the *gist* of it, but not enough to...

2. The jury was shocked when, during the trial, the *dastardly* criminal...

3. Mom would not *bandy* any comments about extending my curfew because she felt that...

4. The *jaded* artist decided to find a new career when...

5. The revolutionaries *effaced* statues of the former dictator because...

6. Mondello the Great *mesmerized* the children at the birthday party by...

7. Someone who *advocates* good manners might become angry if you...

8. The overwhelming *charisma* of the cult leader made it easy for him to...

9. The linebackers on the football team looked like *ogres* compared to...

10. Mom had to explain to Maggie that an imaginary friend is not a real *entity*; it is...

EXERCISE III—Roots, Prefixes, and Suffixes

Study the entries and answer the questions that follow.

The root *fort* means "strong."
The root *graph* means "writing."
The root *gen* means "born," "to produce," or "kind" (type).
The prefix *mono* means "one."

1. Using literal translations as guidance, define the following words without using a dictionary.

   A. generic   D. fort
   B. generate   E. monologue
   C. fortify   F. graphic

2. The coach says that this year, the strong players on the team have the _____ to make it to the championships. The activity that you do best—your strong point—might be called your _____[e].

3. A group of people born within a certain time period is a[n] _____. Your _____ will determine what physical traits you will have.

4. List all the words that you can think of that contain the roots *graph* and *gen*.

EXERCISE IV—Inference

Complete the sentences by inferring information about the italicized word from its context.

1. If you didn't understand the *gist* of the lecture, then you should find the teacher after class and ask...

2. When someone who *advocates* energy conservation sees lights left on, he or she might...

3. If you *efface* your fears about flying, then you might be willing to...

EXERCISE V—Writing

Here is a writing prompt similar to the one you will find on the writing portion of the SAT.

Plan and write an essay based on the following statement:

> The Kites of olden times, as well as the Swans, had the privilege of song. But having heard the neigh of the horse, they were so enchanted with the sound, that they tried to imitate it; and, in trying to neigh, they forgot how to sing.
> –Aesop, Sixth Century B.C.

Assignment: Aesop was a prolific fabulist who used animals to portray roles in his fables. In an essay, explain why Aesop used kites (hawks) and swans to convey the moral lesson of his fable, and then provide a modern explanation of the message. Support your idea with evidence from your reading, classroom studies, experience, and observation.

Thesis: Write a one-sentence response to the assignment. Make certain this single sentence offers a clear statement of your position.

> *Example: In his fable about kites and swans, Aesop is attempting to impart the message that people who automatically follow trends or try to emulate others risk losing their own identities.*

Organizational Plan: If your thesis is the point on which you want to end, where does your essay need to begin? List the points of development that are inevitable in leading your reader from your beginning point to your end point. This is your outline.

Draft: Use your thesis as both your beginning and your end. Following your outline, write a good first draft of your essay. Remember to support all your points with examples, facts, references to reading, etc.

Review and Revise: Exchange essays with a classmate. Using the scoring guide for Sentence Formation and Variety on page 223, score your partner's essay (while he or she scores yours). Focus on sentence structure and use of language conventions. If necessary, rewrite your essay to improve the sentence structure and/or your use of language.

Identifying Sentence Errors

Identify the grammatical error in each of the following sentences. If the sentence contains no error, select answer choice E.

1. Larry <u>said that he</u> had personally <u>designed</u> the web pages with the
           (A)   (B)
   <u>help of himself</u> and <u>his employees</u>.   <u>No error</u>.
   (C)   (D)   (E)

2. <u>I didn't</u> do <u>nothing for the last ten</u> minutes <u>but argue</u>
    (A)   (B)   (C)
   <u>with my sister.</u>   <u>No error</u>
       (D)   (E)

3. <u>Problems with</u> aggressive <u>wildlife often begins</u>
        (A)   (B)
   <u>with aggressive human</u> <u>beings.</u>   <u>No error</u>
         (C)   (D)   (E)

4. <u>Hot and full of sick people,</u> the patients <u>in the front room</u>
          (A)   (B)
   <u>were given</u> their <u>flu shots.</u>   <u>No error</u>
     (C)   (D)   (E)

5. Proponents <u>for the construction</u> of a new intrastate expressway
             (A)
   <u>includes</u> at least four <u>people</u> known <u>to be affiliated</u> with
    (B)   (C)   (D)
   organized crime operations.   <u>No error</u>
                         (E)

Improving Sentences

The underlined portion of each sentence below contains some flaw. Select the answer choice that best corrects the flaw.

6.   The victims were lying on the ground and firemen arrived to douse the flames and take them to the hospital.
     A.   The victims were lying on the ground when firemen arrived to douse the flames and take them to the hospital.
     B.   Fireman arrived to douse the flames and to take the victims lying on the ground to the hospital.
     C.   After dousing the flames on the ground, the firemen took the victims to the hospital.
     D.   Firemen arrived to douse the flames, when victims were lying on the ground, and they were taken to the hospital.
     E.   Victims lying on the ground were taken to the hospital and firemen arrived to douse the flames.

7.   Because of the hurricane warning, everyone sat inside and talked about the game around the dining room table.
     A.   sat inside around the dining room table and talked about the game.
     B.   sat inside the game and talked around the dining room table.
     C.   sat inside the dining room and talked about the table.
     D.   sat and talked inside the game around the table in the dining room.
     E.   talked about the game and sat at the dining room table.

8.   We intend to measure the individual results against its costs.
     A.   against the costs.
     B.   against costs.
     C.   against their costs.
     D.   with their costs.
     E.   against the individual costs.

9.   Deep-sea fishing no longer fascinates me as much as to go to computer demonstrations.
     A.   I am interested in computer demonstrations.
     B.   going to computer demonstrations.
     C.   to go to a computer demonstration.
     D.   computer demonstrations.
     E.   demonstrating computers.

10.　<u>Amadeus Mozart was a brilliant composer he was said to be a little crazy</u>.
   A.　Amadeus Mozart was said to be a little crazy and he was a brilliant composer.
   B.　A brilliant composer Amadeus Mozart was. He was also said to be a little crazy.
   C.　Although a brilliant composer, Amadeus Mozart was said to be a little crazy.
   D.　Although he was said to be a little crazy, Amadeus Mozart was a brilliant composer
   E.　A brilliant composer, although a little crazy, was said to be Amadeus Mozart.

Lesson Six

1. **nepotism** (nep´ ə tiz əm) *n.* favoritism shown to family or friends by those in power, especially in business or hiring practices
I was qualified for the job, but Uncle Mike refused to hire me because he did not want to be accused of *nepotism*.

2. **begrudge** (bi gruj´) *v.* to resent another's success; to envy
Craig, the younger brother, secretly *begrudged* Brian's fortune.
syn: resent   *ant: forgive*

3. **mandarin** (man´ də rin) *n.* an influential person; a member of an elite group
Mandarins and bureaucrats discussed the state of the economy during the summit.

4. **glutinous** (glōōt´ n əs) *adj.* gluey; sticky
The bread dough was in a *glutinous* mass that stuck to anything it touched.

5. **enmity** (en´ mi tē) *n.* deep-seated hostility, often mutual
Angry stares revealed the mutual *enmity* between Steve and his supervisor.
syn: hatred; antagonism   *ant: friendship*

6. **declaim** (di klām´) *v.* to speak in a dramatic, impassioned, or blustering manner
At the debate, each politician *declaimed* against the policies of the others.
syn: trumpet   *ant: whisper*

7. **imbue** (im byōō´) *v.* to inspire or influence; to saturate
Her hard-working mother *imbued* Jane with a solid work ethic.
syn: instill; pervade

8. **gaff** (gaf) *n.* a pole with a large hook on one end
The fisherman used a *gaff* to drag the heavy swordfish onto the boat.

9. **quaff** (kwof) *v.* to drink in large quantities; to gulp
The old captain *quaffed* his ale and then ordered another stein.
syn: guzzle; swig   *ant: sip*

10. **bibliophile** (bib´ lē ə fīl) *n.* a lover of books
The *bibliophile* was thrilled to get a job at the library.

EXERCISE I—Words in Context

From the list below, supply the words needed to complete the paragraph. Some words will not be used.

nepotism	declaim	imbue	begrudged	enmity

1. The _____ between Mike and Brad showed through the manner in which they argued over the most trivial company decisions. Weeks before, Brad had been promoted to regional manager in an obvious act of _____, since his uncle is a member of the board of directors. Mike _____ Brad for the promotion because it had taken fifteen years for Mike to become a regional manager, and Brad had walked into the job with practically no experience at all. Now, during any argument with Brad, Mike was sure to _____ about how "fifteen years of seniority and experience make my decisions practically infallible."

From the list below, supply the words needed to complete the paragraph. Some words will not be used.

nepotism	mandarin	bibliophile	imbue

2. Corporate leaders, high-ranking government officials, and influential _____ gathered in the halls of Xavier's mansion at least once a month. Dinner was held in the ballroom, and then Xavier, a noted _____, usually invited his guests to his colossal private library. Bookshelves towered over the guests, and the presence of hundreds of rare, ancient tomes _____ them with a sense of humility as they stood among the centuries of human thought that had built the world in which they now lived.

From the list below, supply the words needed to complete the paragraph. Some words will not be used.

glutinous	quaff	declaim	gaff

3. When the whaling ship encountered a tiny skiff bobbing on the high seas, the captain ordered a sailor to snag it with a[n] _____. To the sailor's surprise, a sun-beaten man lay on the bottom of the boat. He awoke to the voices of his rescuers, and he immediately _____ the water they offered him. Apparently, the man had kept himself alive by eating the _____ remnants of wet rations that he salvaged before a violent storm sunk his ship.

EXERCISE II—Sentence Completion

Complete the sentence in a way that shows you understand the meaning of the italicized vocabulary word.

1.   During a break from toiling in the oppressive heat, the workers *quaffed*...

2.   Dad spent all day fixing the car and then *declaimed* that...

3.   The man working in the reptile exhibit used a *gaff* to...

4.   Some parents accused the coach of *nepotism* because...

5.   Working on a farm *imbued* Mary with...

6.   The activists wanted Dorian's support because he is a *mandarin* who can...

7.   You knew that Frank was a *bibliophile* because...

8.   The scientist said that the *glutinous* substance had similar characteristics to...

9.   There was *enmity* between the brother and sister ever since...

10.   Gloria secretly *begrudged* her friend...

EXERCISE III—Roots, Prefixes, and Suffixes

Study the entries and answer the questions that follow.

The prefix *biblio* means "book."
The root *mort* means "death."
The roots *voc* and *vok* mean "to call."

1. Using literal translations as guidance, define the following words without using a dictionary.

    A. bibliography   D. vocation
    B. biblical   E. vociferous
    C. mortician   F. mortuary

2. If you get too many speeding tickets, the department of transportation might call back, or _____, your driver's license. An *advocate* is someone who _____ a particular cause.

3. List as many words as you can think of that contain the roots *mort, voc,* and *vok.*

EXERCISE IV—Inference

Complete the sentences by inferring information about the italicized word from its context.

1. *Nepotism* is common in family businesses, where many of the employees are hired because they…

2. Kelly attributed her artistic success to the fact that her mentor had *imbued* her with…

3. If people avoid you because you always *declaim* your own skills, then you should probably learn to…

EXERCISE V—Critical Reading

Below is a reading passage followed by several multiple-choice questions similar to the ones you will encounter on the SAT. Carefully read the passage and choose the best answer for each of the questions.

The following passage is an adaptation of a letter written in 1904 by President Theodore Roosevelt. Roosevelt is remembered for his limitless energy, his aggressive foreign and domestic policies, his economic reform, and his often-militant patriotic fervor. The passage reveals a side of Roosevelt of which many citizens were unaware.

Dear Ted:

This will be a long business letter. I sent to you the examination papers for West Point and Annapolis. I have thought a great deal over the matter, and discussed it at great length with Mother. I feel on the one hand that I ought to give you my best advice, and yet on the other hand I do not wish to seem to constrain
5   you against your wishes. If you have definitely made up your mind that you have an overmastering desire to be in the Navy or the Army, and that such a career is the one in which you will take a really heart-felt interest—far more so than any other—and that your greatest chance for happiness and usefulness will lie in doing this one work to which you feel yourself especially drawn—why, under
10   such circumstances, I have but little to say. But I am not satisfied that this is really your feeling. It seemed to me more as if you did not feel drawn in any other direction, and wondered what you were going to do in life or what kind of work you would turn your hand to, and wondered if you could make a success or not; and that you are therefore inclined to turn to the Navy or Army chiefly because
15   you would then have a definite and settled career in life, and could hope to go on steadily without any great risk of failure. Now, if such is your thought, I shall quote to you what Captain Mahan said of his son when asked why he did not send him to West Point or Annapolis. "I have too much confidence in him to make me feel that it is desirable for him to enter either branch of the service."
20   I have great confidence in you. I believe you have the ability and, above all, the energy, the perseverance, and the common sense, to win out in civil life. That you will have some hard times and some discouraging times I have no question; but this is merely another way of saying that you will share the common lot. Though you will have to work in different ways from those in which I worked,
25   you will not have to work any harder, nor to face periods of more discouragement. I trust in your ability, and especially your character, and I am confident you will win.

In the Army and the Navy the chance for a man to show great ability and rise above his fellows does not occur on the average more than once in a generation.
30   When I was down at Santiago it was melancholy for me to see how fossilized and lacking in ambition, and generally useless, were most of the men of my age and over, who had served their lives in the Army. The Navy for the last few years has

35 been better, but for twenty years after the Civil War there was less chance in the Navy than in the Army to practice, and do, work of real consequence. I have actually known lieutenants in both the Army and the Navy who were grandfathers—men who had seen their children married before they themselves attained the grade of captain. Of course the chance may come at any time when the man of West Point or Annapolis who will have stayed in the Army or Navy finds a great war on, and therefore has the opportunity to rise high. Under such circum-

40 stances, I think that the man of such training who has actually left the Army or the Navy has even more chance of rising than the man who has remained in it. Moreover, often a man can do as I did in the Spanish War, even though not a West-Pointer. This last point raises the question about you going to West Point or Annapolis and leaving the Army or Navy after you have served the regulation

45 four years (I think that is the number) after graduation from the academy. Under this plan you would have an excellent education and a grounding in discipline and, in some ways, a testing of your capacity greater than I think you can get in any ordinary college. On the other hand, except for the profession of an engineer, you would have had nothing like special training, and you would be so ordered

50 about, and arranged for, that you would have less independence of character than you could gain from them. You would have had fewer temptations; but you would have had less chance to develop the qualities which overcome temptations and show that a man has individual initiative. Supposing you entered at seventeen, with the intention of following this course. The result would be that at

55 twenty-five you would leave the Army or Navy without having gone through any law school or any special technical school of any kind, and would start your life work three or four years later than your schoolfellows of today, who go to work immediately after leaving college. Of course, under such circumstances, you might study law, for instance, during the four years after graduation; but my own

60 feeling is that a man does good work chiefly when he is in something which he intends to make his permanent work, and in which he is deeply interested. Moreover, there will always be the chance that the number of officers in the Army or Navy will be deficient, and that you would have to stay in the service instead of getting out when you wished.

65 I want you to think over all these matters very seriously. It would be a great misfortune for you to start into the Army or Navy as a career, and find that you had mistaken your desires and had gone in without really weighing the matter. You ought not to enter unless you feel genuinely drawn to the life as a life-work. If so, go in; but not otherwise.

70 Mr. Loeb told me today that at seventeen he had tried for the army, but failed. The competitor who beat him in is now a captain; Mr. Loeb has passed him by, although meanwhile a war has been fought. Mr. Loeb says he wished to enter the army because he did not know what to do, could not foresee whether he would succeed or fail in life, and felt the army would give him "a living and a career."

75 Now if this is at bottom your feeling I should advise you not to go in; I should say yes to some boys, but not to you; I believe in you too much, and have too much confidence in you.

1. The passage is a letter from a
    A. mother to a daughter.
    B. uncle to a nephew.
    C. father to a son.
    D. teacher to a student.
    E. president to a relative.

2. Which of the following best describes the purpose of the passage?
    A. describe
    B. entertain
    C. analyze
    D. persuade
    E. inform

3. According to the author, Ted wants to attend military school because
    A. he knows that the military will provide opportunities for success.
    B. he doesn't know what he wants to do, but he wants a steady career.
    C. he wants a steady career that offers more excitement than college.
    D. his father was a war hero who became president.
    E. Captain Mahan told Ted that he would have potential as an officer.

4. According to the author of the passage, participating in a war is
    A. detrimental, because of the risk.
    B. an opportunity to succeed.
    C. character-building, because it provides better challenges than college.
    D. good for professional soldiers, but not sailors.
    E. not a good idea for people who want to be promoted.

5. Which of the following is *not* a reason why a military education followed by a short career would be beneficial?
    A. The military helps to develop discipline.
    B. Military schools provide excellent educations.
    C. The military would prepare a student for a political career.
    D. A military engineer would have the special training for a civilian career.
    E. The military would provide challenges unavailable to civilians.

6. Which best paraphrases the following quotation? (lines 59-61)

> "...my own feeling is that a man does good work chiefly when he is in something which he intends to make his permanent work, and in which he is deeply interested."

   A. People who do not choose the right career just have to learn to deal with it.
   B. Decide what you want to do before committing your life to a career.
   C. Choose your career based on what you want to do for the rest of your life.
   D. People do their best work when they love what they are doing.
   E. Choosing a career path should depend on how much glory you need.

7. As used in line 63, *deficient* most nearly means
   A. lacking.
   B. deployed.
   C. captured.
   D. defective
   E. improper.

8. According to the passage, the existence of temptation is
   A. dangerous because it can lead to imprisonment in the military.
   B. good because it provokes thought.
   C. not covered in the letter.
   D. necessary because it separates the good from the bad.
   E. good because it inspires resistance and individuality.

9. Mr. Loeb was Roosevelt's advisor. The mention of Loeb's story in the final paragraph suggests which of the following?
   A. People can achieve as much success as civilians as they can as members of the military.
   B. Loeb was lucky to become a presidential advisor.
   C. People should enlist in the Navy, not the Army.
   D. People who do not make Captain should get leave the Army because they can get better civilian careers.
   E. People who lack confidence will not succeed in the military.

10. The tone of this passage is best described as
   A. anxious and judgmental.
   B. panicked and bossy.
   C. concerned and supportive.
   D. serious and demanding.
   E. pleased and affectionate.

Lesson Seven

1. **gird** (gûrd) *v.* to prepare for an event or an action
   Residents of the shore *girded* themselves for the upcoming hurricane.
   syn: brace

2. **daunt** (dônt) *v.* to make afraid; to discourage
   The high waves and the approaching storm did not *daunt* the treasure hunters.
   syn: intimidate; dishearten   *ant: encourage*

3. **flux** (fluks) *n.* a state of continual change or movement
   The constant *flux* of the stock market now makes investing risky.
   syn: fluctuation; instability   *ant: stability; solidity*

4. **hovel** (hov´əl) *n.* a wretched living place; an open shed
   The child welfare agent removed the children from the filthy *hovel*.
   syn: shanty; shack   *ant: palace; mansion*

5. **cadaverous** (kə dav´ ər əs) *adj.* of or like a corpse; pale, gaunt, thin
   The old pirate's *cadaverous* face made the young sailor tremble.
   syn: ghastly   *ant: robust; healthy*

6. **gothic** (goth´ ik) *adj.* of the middle ages; of or relating to a
       mysterious, grotesque, and desolate style of fiction
   A romantic story line offset some of the dreary and gloomy elements of the *gothic* novel.

7. **penury** (pen´ yə rē) *n.* extreme poverty
   Though born into *penury,* he became one of the country's wealthiest entrepreneurs.
   syn: destitution   *ant: wealth; opulence*

8. **egress** (ē´ gres) *n.* an exit; a means of going out
   The only *egress* on the submarine was the main hatch on the tower.
   syn: passage   *ant: ingress; entrance*

9. **felicity** (fə lis´ i tē) *n.* happiness; bliss
   Rose mistakenly thought that her wealth ensured *felicity*, but she quickly learned that money does not buy happiness.
   syn: euphoria; delight   *ant: unhappiness; discontent*

10. **despot** (des´ pət) *n.* a dictator with absolute power
    During his rule, Stalin was a despot responsible for the death of millions of his own people.
    syn: tyrant

EXERCISE I—Words in Context

From the list below, supply the words needed to complete the paragraph. Some words will not be used.

flux	hovel	despot	gird
egress	cadaverous	penury	

1. When the _____ assassinated the monarch and seized control of the government, the already poor nation became one of abject _____. The majority of citizens lived in poorly maintained _____ that would likely be condemned by the standards of most other nations. Starvation and epidemics turned what should have been healthy, young workers into _____ zombies who hoped to have enough energy to scrounge for roots to feed their families. Citizens had only two means of _____ from the misery—through the demilitarized zone or across the border into China. Escape was a risky undertaking; if captured, refugees faced imprisonment or execution.

From the list below, supply the words needed to complete the paragraph. Some words will not be used.

felicity	penury	gird	flux
daunt	gothic	hovel	

2. Despite their tremendous destructive power, tornadoes do not _____ the Russell family; they have experienced too many storms even to care. The weather conditions of the Midwest are in constant _____, and the family seldom allows adverse weather to detract from the _____ of their day-to-day lives. Their underground shelter might resemble a[n] _____ dungeon, but for the Russells, it is a place to sit out the storm and listen to Mr. Russell's stories about how he weathered storms during his childhood. He often relates the day in which a tornado passed while he was far from shelter, and he and his parents _____ themselves for the oncoming storm.

EXERCISE II—Sentence Completion

Complete the sentence in a way that shows you understand the meaning of the italicized vocabulary word.

1. The family lived a life of *penury* after...

2. The children exhibited total *felicity* while...

3. The *gothic* architecture of the castle is characteristic of...

4. Don't let the size of the players *daunt* you; they're not...

5. Linda *girded* herself against the swarm of killer bees by...

6. When Connie saw the *cadaverous* refugees, she immediately...

7. The wealthy industrialist was born in a *hovel*, but he...

8. If Amy had not found an *egress* from the burning house, she...

9. Because of the *flux* of customers, Sal didn't know if her restaurant would...

10. The *despot* ordered his guards to...

EXERCISE III—Roots, Prefixes, and Suffixes

Study the entries and answer the questions that follow.

The suffix *ism* means "belief in."
The root *deci* means "ten."
The prefix *anti* means "against."
The roots *duc* and *duct* mean "to lead."
The root *do* means "to give."

1.   *Using literal translations as guidance, define the following words without using a dictionary.*

   A. idealism   D. objectivism
   B. abduct   E. duct
   C. donate   F. pardon

2.   A medicine that works against certain symptoms by taking them away is called a[n] _____. A battleship might have _____ guns for use against enemy planes.

3.   A[n] _____ is a ten-year period, and the word that originally meant "to kill every tenth person" is _____.

4.   List as many words as you can think of that contain the roots *duc* or *duct*.

EXERCISE IV—Inference

Complete the sentences by inferring information about the italicized word from its context.

1.   In order to elicit a confession, a detective might try to *daunt* an overconfident suspect by…

2.   A homeless person living in *penury* would probably appreciate…

3.   If a city experiences a *flux* in population, then people are…

EXERCISE V—Writing

Here is a writing prompt similar to the one you will find on the writing portion of the SAT.

Plan and write an essay on the following statement:

It was one of the significant declarations of an English critic and moralist who said that conduct is three fourths of life. A writer on psychology said that three fourths of our daily conduct consists in simply taking off the brakes and letting ideas and impulses have their way.
–Anna Harris Smith
Golden Words for Daily Counsel, 1888

Assignment: Anna Harris Smith wrote this passage for a book that offers guidance for day-to-day life, but the two references seem to be contradictory. Do you agree with the first premise, the second premise, or a combination of the two? In an essay, explain which solution you favor as the ideal guidance for daily living. Support your position with evidence from your reading, classroom studies, experience, and observation.

Thesis Write a one-sentence response to the assignment. Make certain this single sentence offers a clear statement of your position.

Example: The philosophy of the moralist, that conduct is three fourths of life, is correct because the average person must interact with other people most of the day, and any interaction is conduct.

Organizational Plan: If your thesis is the point on which you want to end, where does your essay need to begin? List the points of development that are inevitable in leading your reader from your beginning point to your end point. This list is your outline.

Draft: Use your thesis as both your beginning and your end. Following your outline, write a good first draft of your essay. Remember to support all your points with examples, facts, references to reading, etc.

Review and Revise: Exchange essays with a classmate. Use the scoring guide for Word Choice on page 224 to score your partner's essay (while he or she scores yours). Focus on the word choice and use of language conventions. If necessary, rewrite your essay to improve the word choice and/or your use of language.

Improving Paragraphs

Read the following passage and then answer the multiple-choice questions that follow. The questions will require you to make decisions regarding the revision of the reading selection.

(1) Plaid may not be exactly what you think it is. (2) Tartan may be what you think plaid is.

(3) Autumn usually finds us wrapped in a tartan, whether they are around our torsos, our legs, or a combination of both. (4) The use of a "plaid" seems to come into fashion every autumn and can be a handsome addition to any outfit. (5) Warmth is a bonus of wearing a plaid, no matter what design it is.

(6) A plaid, you see, is a woven piece of fabric worn over the shoulder sometimes tucked under a belt to hold it in place. (7) The design of various colored stripes crossing at right angles is rightfully a tartan, many a plaid is a tartan design.

(8) The autumn is a great time of the year to purchase a favorite tartan and sew a lovely long skirt for informal entertaining at home. (9) The closet must be full of soft old shirts of particular tartans to wrap around our shoulders for a quick trip to the post office. (10) The design is an old favorite for ties and scarves, lap robes and carriage covers for baby's stroller. (11) Some believe that the tartan design originated as a way to incorporate expensive, dyed threads in cheap materials. (12) No matter what you choose to tailor, it is guaranteed to be an eye-catching, original design.

(13) If you have a yen for pretty colors and patterns with classic lines, feel free to make yourself a plaid with knotted tassels on the edge. (14) Wear it for warmth and style as you enjoy the autumn weather. (15) If you have a fear of tying, then buy a huge tartan scarf and throw it over your shoulder with a flair for flamboyance.

1. Which of the following suggestions would improve the development of the beginning of the passage?
    A. Exchange paragraphs 1 and 3.
    B. Exchange paragraphs 2 and 3.
    C. Exchange paragraphs 3 and 1.
    D. Exchange paragraphs 1 and 2.
    E. Make no changes in the first 3 paragraphs.

2. Which of the following describes the error in paragraph 2?
    A. run-on sentence
    B. spelling error
    C. sentence fragment
    D. improper pronoun agreement
    E. incorrect prepositional phrase

3. Which of the following would correct the error in paragraph 3?
    A. Combine sentences 6 and 7.
    B. Capitalize *tartan*.
    C. Make two sentences out of sentence 6.
    D. Delete *you see*.
    E. Add *and* after the comma in sentence 7.

4. Which of the following should be deleted from paragraph 4?
    A. sentence 8
    B. sentence 9
    C. sentence 10
    D. sentence 11
    E. sentence 12

5. Which of the following changes would best improve the concluding paragraph?
    A. Reverse the order of the sentences.
    B. Exchange sentences 13 and 14.
    C. Exchange sentences 14 and 15.
    D. Make no change.
    E. Delete the paragraph.

REVIEW

Lessons 1 – 7

EXERCISE I – Sentence Completion

Choose the best pair of words to complete the sentence. Most choices will fit grammatically and will even make sense logically, but you must choose the pair that best fits the idea of the sentence.

Note that these words are not taken directly from lessons in this book. This exercise is intended to replicate the sentence completion portion of the SAT.

1. There must have been a[n] _____ in the calendars; one said Mother's Day fell on a Tuesday, but the other had the holiday _____ on Wednesday.
   A. discrepancy, next
   B. problem, disappear
   C. glitch, fall
   D. fault, marked
   E. coincidence, appear

2. Within the fugitive's hideout, unseen by the _____, lay a masterful, _____ array of booby traps, which protected the entire area against any incursion.
   A. predators, complicated
   B. family, deadly
   C. captors, vast
   D. seekers, infrared
   E. pursuers, labyrinthine

3. It was _____ to the dictator that he was respected; his only concern was that his _____ was feared.
   A. important, omnipotence
   B. bothersome, regime
   C. unknown, whim
   D. manifest, vengeance
   E. immaterial, authority

4. Just as the horse and carriage did, some day the automobile will also find its way onto the heap of _____ curiosities, when its efficiency is _____ by another advance in technology.
   A. quaint, decreased
   B. obsolete, supplanted
   C. unreliable, diminished
   D. impotent, superseded
   E. old-fashioned, regulated

5. If there were no standard by which to measure the _____ of tornadoes, meteorologists would have to _____ one.
   A. winds, complete
   B. strength, devise
   C. destruction, compile
   D. duration, improvise
   E. location, implement

6. _____ with the police was the most _____ way for the criminal to receive better treatment.
   A. Collaborating, clever
   B. Cooperating, efficient
   C. Talking, sensitive
   D. Communicating, assuring
   E. Maneuvering, effective

7. Throughout the office, employees seemed to be in a complete state of _____ whenever the boss _____ a new project.
   A. confusion, unveiled
   B. tumult, planned
   C. acclamation, desired
   D. relaxation, conceived
   E. disorder, needed

8. Despite the horticulturist's best efforts, the plant _____ and died in the _____ summer sun.
   A. shrunk, incredible
   B. decayed, moderate
   C. thrived, sunny
   D. shriveled, blazing
   E. wasted, seasonal

EXERCISE II – Crossword Puzzle

Use the clues to complete the crossword puzzle. The answers consist of vocabulary words from lessons 1 through 7.

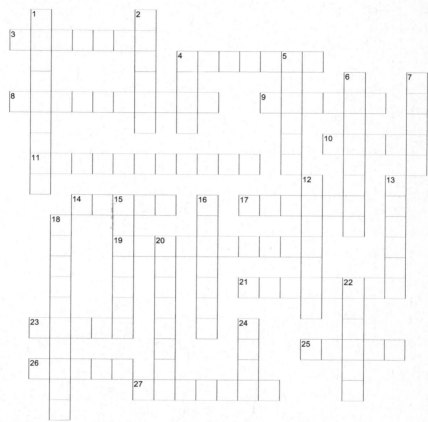

Across
3. occupant; inhabitant
4. to please
8. an exaggerated portrayal
9. in high spirits
10. dirty, wretched living place
11. promoting equal rights
14. to inspire or influence
17. exit; means of going out
19. morally unrestrained
21. to resent another's success
23. worn out; dulled
25. to escape notice
26. to make afraid; to discourage
27. scarcity; lack

Down
1. to besiege by encircling
2. deep-seated hostility
4. to prepare for an event
5. inactive; unproductive
6. favoritism shown to family or friends
7. to waste time
12. in a state of violent rage
13. to wipe out
15. delayed
16. dreamily thoughtful
18. to combine
20. personal appeal; magnetism
22. to mislead; to fool
24. main point

Lesson Eight

1. **beget** (bi get´) v. to produce; to make happen
   Hatred *begets* more hatred.
   syn: generate   *ant: prevent*

2. **educe** (i dōōs´) v. to draw or bring out
   The lawyer tried to *educe* a response from the witness.
   syn: elicit   *ant: suppress*

3. **glean** (glēn) v. to collect bit by bit; to gather with patient labor
   The investigator *gleaned* pertinent information from the witnesses to the crash.
   syn: garner   *ant: disperse*

4. **chafe** (chāf) v. to wear or irritate, often through rubbing or friction
   The freezing wind *chafed* our faces as we struggled through the storm.

5. **effrontery** (i frun´ tə rē) n. shameless boldness
   The thief had the *effrontery* to demand a reward for returning the money he had stolen.
   syn: impudence; nerve; audacity   *ant: timidity*

6. **imbibe** (im bīb´) v. to drink (especially alcohol)
   After the raid, the Vikings feasted and *imbibed* to the point of physical sickness.

7. **feign** (fān) v. to pretend
   He *feigned* an interest in the conversation, but his mind wandered elsewhere.
   syn: simulate; fake

8. **desist** (di sist´) v. to stop; discontinue
   The police ordered the rioters to *desist* before someone got hurt.
   syn: cease; end   *ant: begin; start*

9. **allude** (ə lōōd´) v. to hint at, to refer to indirectly
   The attorney *alluded* to a cover-up without actually mentioning it.
   syn: suggest; imply   *ant: expose*

10. **elite** (e lēt´) n. the choice members or best of a group
    Soldiers in the Special Forces are part of the military's *elite*.
    syn: leaders   *ant: common; multitude*

EXERCISE I—Words in Context

From the list below, supply the words needed to complete the paragraph. Some words will not be used.

beget	imbibe	chafe	feign
desist	glean	effrontery	educe

1. The psychologist used a form of hypnotism to _____ her patient's childhood memories. Little by little, the doctor _____ clues that might _____ the solution to Kate's disorder. Originally, the doctor worried that Kate would _____ compliance and simply pretend to remember things, but the doctor could tell that the memories were real by the way in which they seemed to _____ the patient emotionally. One hour was all Kate could stand before her therapy had to _____ for the day.

From the list below, supply the words needed to complete the paragraph. Some words will not be used.

effrontery	beget	elite
imbibe	allude	

2. As usual, the Senator's cocktail party was a gathering of the society _____. Some guests mingled and chatted about politics while they _____ fine wine, but others demonstrated a social _____ by first eating and then criticizing the host's menu selections. The critics never actually said they didn't enjoy the food, of course; they merely _____ to the host's questionable choice of caterer.

EXERCISE II—Sentence Completion

Complete the sentence in a way that shows you understand the meaning of the italicized vocabulary word.

1. The councilman was concerned that a pool hall would *beget*…

2. Members of the school's academic *elite* were chosen to…

3. From her moving story, the author hoped that readers would *educe*…

4. Without actually saying what was wrong with the program, Beth *alluded* to…

5. Jaime *gleaned* as much information about painting as she could before she…

6. The teacher told the students that if they didn't *desist*, they would…

7. The criminal complained that his handcuffs *chafed*…

8. Neil *feigned* sickness in an effort to…

9. In a display of *effrontery*, the waiter…

10. The festive bunch feasted and *imbibed* after…

EXERCISE III—Roots, Prefixes, and Suffixes

Study the entries and answer the questions that follow.

The root *termin* means "end" or "boundary."
The root *ver* means "true."
The roots *dem* and *demos* mean "people."

1. *Using literal translations as guidance, define the following words without using a dictionary.*

    A. terminal   D. verify
    B. terminate   E. verdict
    C. exterminate   F. democracy

2. When many people contract a disease, it is said to be a[n] _____.
    If *gogue* means "to lead," then a *demagogue* is _____.

3. List as many words as you can think of that contain the root *term*.

EXERCISE IV—Inference

Complete the sentences by inferring information about the italicized word from its context.

1. If someone *feigns* sleep, then he or she…

2. Someone who is afraid to tell you something might instead *allude* to…

3. If the school wants a particular activity to *desist*, it must want…

EXERCISE V—Critical Reading

Below is a pair of reading passages followed by several multiple-choice questions similar to the ones you will encounter on the SAT. Carefully read both passages and choose the best answer to each of the questions.

The first passage is an excerpt from Rebecca Harding Davis's <u>Life In The Iron Mills</u>, *a description of life and living conditions during the early stages of American industry. The second passage is an excerpt from Charles Dickens's* <u>Hard Times</u>, *a Victorian novel set in the fictional industrial city of Coketown, England.*

Passage 1

A CLOUDY DAY: do you know what that is in a town of iron-works? The sky sank down before dawn, muddy, flat, immovable. The air is thick, clammy with the breath of crowded human beings. It stifles me. I open the window, and, look-ing out, can scarcely see through the rain the grocer's shop opposite, where a
5   crowd of drunken Irishmen are puffing Lynchburg tobacco in their pipes. I can detect the scent through all the foul smells ranging loose in the air.

The idiosyncrasy of this town is smoke. It rolls sullenly in slow folds from the great chimneys of the iron-founderies, and settles down in black, slimy pools on the muddy streets. Smoke on the wharves, smoke on the dingy boats, on the
10   yellow river,—clinging in a coating of greasy soot to the house-front, the two faded poplars, the faces of the passers-by. The long train of mules, dragging mass-es of pig-iron through the narrow street, have a foul vapor hanging to their reek-ing sides. Here, inside, is a little broken figure of an angel pointing upward from the mantel-shelf; but even its wings are covered with smoke, clotted and black.
15   Smoke everywhere! A dirty canary chirps desolately in a cage beside me. Its dream of green fields and sunshine is a very old dream,—almost worn out, I think.

From the back-window I can see a narrow brick-yard sloping down to the river-side, strewed with rain-butts and tubs. The river, dull and tawny-colored,
20   (*la belle riviere!*) drags itself sluggishly along, tired of the heavy weight of boats and coal-barges. What wonder? When I was a child, I used to fancy a look of weary, dumb appeal upon the face of the negro-like river slavishly bearing its burden day after day. Something of the same idle notion comes to me to-day, when from the street-window I look on the slow stream of human life creeping
25   past, night and morning, to the great mills. Masses of men, with dull, besotted faces bent to the ground, sharpened here and there by pain or cunning; skin and muscle and flesh begrimed with smoke and ashes; stooping all night over boiling caldrons of metal, laired by day in dens of drunkenness and infamy; breathing from infancy to death an air saturated with fog and grease and soot, vileness for
30   soul and body. What do you make of a case like that, amateur psychologist? You call it an altogether serious thing to be alive: to these men it is a drunken jest, a joke,—horrible to angels perhaps, to them commonplace enough. My fancy

about the river was an idle one: it is no type of such a life. What if it be stagnant and slimy here? It knows that beyond there waits for it odorous sunlight,—
35 quaint old gardens, dusky with soft, green foliage of apple-trees, and flushing crimson with roses,—air, and fields, and mountains. The future of the Welsh puddler passing just now is not so pleasant. To be stowed away, after his grimy work is done, in a hole in the muddy graveyard, and after that,—*not* air, nor green fields, nor curious roses.

Passage 2

It was a town of red brick, or of brick that would have been red if the smoke and ashes had allowed it; but as matters stood it was a town of unnatural red and black like the painted face of a savage. It was a town of machinery and tall chimneys, out of which interminable serpents of smoke trailed themselves for ever
5   and ever, and never got uncoiled. It had a black canal in it, and a river that ran purple with ill-smelling dye, and vast piles of building full of windows where there was a rattling and a trembling all day long, and where the piston of the steam-engine worked monotonously up and down like the head of an elephant in a state of melancholy madness. It contained several large streets all very like
10 one another, and many small streets still more like one another, inhabited by people equally like one another, who all went in and out at the same hours, with the same sound upon the same pavements, to do the same work, and to whom every day was the same as yesterday and tomorrow, and every year the counterpart of the last and the next.
15 These attributes of Coketown were in the main inseparable from the work by which it was sustained; against them were to be set off, comforts of life which found their way all over the world, and elegancies of life which made, we will not ask how much of the fine lady, who could scarcely bear to hear the place mentioned.

1.   The overall tone of the first passage can best be described as
      A. joyous.
      B. nostalgic.
      C. disheartening.
      D. ironic.
      E. condemning.

2.   As used in paragraph 2 of the first passage, *idiosyncrasy* most nearly
      means
      A. downfall.
      B. savior.
      C. dogma.
      D. quirk.
      E. transformation.

3.   What is the author's intention for personifying smoke in the second para-
      graph of passage 1?
      A. to describe the pollution of the town
      B. to emphasize the annoying effects of the smoke
      C. to introduce the smoke as a character
      D. to make the smoke appear benevolent
      E. to describe the town from the smoke's point of view

4.   As a child, the author of the first passage imagined the river to have a
      "weary, dumb appeal." What does the author look upon in the same way
      as an adult?
      A. the mill town
      B. the people walking to and from work
      C. the smoke rolling into the town
      D. the grocer's shop
      E. the canary

5.   Why, according to the first passage, does the river have a better life than
      the people of the town?
      A. The river does not have to work in the iron mills.
      B. The Welsh puddler uses the river for transportation.
      C. The river is water and cleanses itself of the pollution.
      D. The people of the town depend on the river for life.
      E. The river must only pass through the town, not live there.

6. The author of the second passage probably uses the simile in line 3 to
    A. convey the author's dislike of savages.
    B. imply that savages are employed as plant workers.
    C. describe the way in which the smoke drifts.
    D. contradict the industrial setting with primitive imagery.
    E. suggest that Coketown is a colony of England.

7. Which of the following best paraphrases lines 9 -14 of the second passage?
    A. The monotonous town had no unique people or characteristics.
    B. Coketown had good days and bad days.
    C. Time passed slowly in the town.
    D. All people enjoyed equal treatment in the town.
    E. Coketown was very orderly.

8. According to both passages, which is a characteristic of the residents of industrial towns?
    A. People use the rivers to get to work.
    B. The people have no hope of leaving the town.
    C. The people live routine lives in unhealthy environments.
    D. The people in both passages work in the same factory.
    E. Most of the people have soot on their faces.

9. Which of the following is not an element of setting shared by both passages?
    A. workers
    B. rivers
    C. canals
    D. chimneys
    E. smoke

10. Which of the following best describes a difference in theme between the two passages?
    A. Passage 1 is about nature, and passage 2 is about social class.
    B. Passage 1 is about industry, while passage 2 is about colonization.
    C. Passage 1 is about pollution, and passage 2 is about slavery.
    D. Passage 1 is about acceptance, and passage 2 is about industry.
    E. Passage 1 is about social class, and passage 2 is about wealth.

Lesson Nine

1. **bilk** (bilk) *v.* to cheat or swindle; to thwart
The landscapers tried to *bilk* the homeowner out of money by charging for work that was never authorized.
syn: defraud; con

2. **homily** (hom´ ə lē) *n.* a sermon
"Sir," I said, "If I may interrupt you, I need food and clothing for these people, not a *homily* on patience."
syn: lecture; speech

3. **demise** (di mīz´) *n.* death; a ceasing to exist
Mary will inherit the estate upon the *demise* of Uncle Irving.
syn: termination; conclusion

4. **emit** (i mit´) *v.* to send out; to give forth, as in sound or light
The lamp did not *emit* enough light for reading.
syn: produce; discharge; release

5. **decadence** (dek´ ə dəns) *n.* moral deterioration
It is often suggested that Rome fell as a result of its own *decadence*.
syn: decay; corruption; debauchery　　　　　　*ant: decency*

6. **aghast** (ə gast´) *adj.* feeling great dismay or horror
We were *aghast* when we saw the disrespectful manner in which the teenager treated her parents.
syn: terrified; horrified; shocked

7. **granary** (gran´ ə rē) *n.* a storehouse for grain
We lost a year's supply of corn when the *granary* burned down.

8. **choleric** (kol´ ə rik) *adj.* easily angered
He was a *choleric* man, whose temper often got him into trouble.
syn: irascible; cantankerous　　　　　　*ant: apathetic; impassive*

9. **impede** (im pēd´) *v.* to hinder, obstruct
The reckless fan's running through the outfield *impeded* the playoff game.
syn: delay; retard　　　　　　*ant: aid; encourage*

10. **qualm** (kwäm) *n.* a feeling of uneasiness
The boy had no *qualms* about cheating on the test.
syn: misgiving　　　　　　*ant: ease*

11. **lampoon** (lam pōōn´) *n.* a written satire used to ridicule or attack
        someone
     The *lampoon* of the athletic program in the school newspaper angered the
     players and the coach.
     syn: parody; caricature

12. **narcissistic** (när si sis´ tic) *adj.* conceited; having excessive self-love
        or admiration
     The *narcissistic* criminal cared only about his own fate.
     syn: vain; egotistic   *ant: humble; modest*

13. **eradicate** (i rad´ i kāt) *v.* to wipe out; to destroy
     The pest control specialist *eradicated* the termites in our house.
     syn: eliminate   *ant: add; create*

14. **fabricate** (fab´ ri kāt) *v.* to concoct; to make up a story in order to
        deceive
     The scientist's career ended when someone discovered that he had *fabri-
     cated* his experiments.
     syn: forge; fake

15. **ghastly** (gast´ lē) *adj.* horrible; frightful
     The *ghastly* smile on the dead man at the end of the movie showed that
     he had enjoyed the last laugh.

     syn: dreadful; hideous   *ant: lovely; attractive*

EXERCISE I—Words in Context

From the list below, supply the words needed to complete the paragraph. Some words will not be used.

decadence	homily	bilk	fabricate
choleric	qualm	narcissistic	

1. The reverend had _____ what he thought was an excellent story for his weekly _____. It was a lengthy parable about a wealthy family that lived in _____ and had no _____ about its lavish lifestyle or mistreatment of servants. The sermon went fairly well until the _____ preacher angrily stopped in mid-sentence to lecture a sleeping member of the congregation.

From the list below, supply the words needed to complete the paragraph. Some words will not be used.

impede	lampoon	demise	granary
ghastly	emit	qualm	

2. Bill arrived at the _____ with his truckload of wheat and with a[n] _____ look on his face. Apparently, the railroad crossing lights had failed to _____ a signal, and Bill had stopped just in time to postpone his _____. The next time he has to drive over railroad tracks, Bill declares, he is going to stop his truck and look both ways, even if he _____ the flow of traffic.

From the list below, supply the words needed to complete the paragraph. Some words will not be used.

narcissistic	decadence	eradicate	bilk
lampoon	aghast	choleric	

3. The author claimed that her article was fiction, but it was actually a[n] _____ that satirized the life of a famous Hollywood figure. It portrayed the famous director as being so _____ that he had mirrors in every room of his mansion so that he could observe his own "perfection" at any given moment. It also portrayed the movie mogul as someone who _____ investors out of their money by knowingly creating box-office failures while pocketing millions. The director was _____ when he read the derisive-but-truthful satire of himself. Within minutes, he was on the phone with his lawyers trying to stop the magazine before the article _____ whatever remained of his credibility.

EXERCISE II—Sentence Completion

Complete the sentence in a way that shows you understand the meaning of the italicized vocabulary word.

1. The gauge on the dashboard *emits* a red light when...

2. If the *granary* fills up too early, the farmers will have to...

3. The late night show included *lampoons* meant to...

4. Larry had no *qualms* about...

5. During the *homily*, Jonathan Edwards warned the congregation that...

6. The *demise* of the old West can be attributed to...

7. The *choleric* sailor often found himself in the brig for...

8. *Narcissistic* people seldom worry about...

9. You could tell by the *ghastly* look on her face that she...

10. Some of the games at the carnival are designed to *bilk* people by...

11. You will *impede* the healing of your broken foot if you...

12. *Decadence* among government officials ultimately caused...

13. You will be *aghast* when you see...

14. Dan tried to *eradicate*...

15. Heidi *fabricated* an excuse for...

EXERCISE III—Roots, Prefixes, and Suffixes

Study the entries and answer the questions that follow.

The root *multi* means "many."
The roots *naut* and *naus* mean "sailor" or "ship."
The roots *nov* and *neo* mean "new."

1. Using literal translations as guidance, define the following words without using a dictionary.

    A. innovation   D. multitude
    B. novel   E. multimedia
    C. nautical   F. neoclassical

2. Someone who is new at a sport is said to be a[n] _____. If you restore an old house to new condition, then you _____ it.

3. Someone who is not used to sailing might get _____, or seasick, on his or her first voyage. A sailor explores or travels the seas, but a[n] _____ travels through space.

4. List as many words as you can think of that contain the roots *multi* and *nov*.

EXERCISE IV—Inference

Complete the sentences by inferring information about the italicized word from its context.

1. A *narcissistic* person might refuse to help someone because...

2. If you have *qualms* about doing something, then you might...

3. People who cannot control their wants and pursue lives of *decadence* are in danger of...

EXERCISE V—Writing

Here is a writing prompt similar to the one you will find on the writing portion of the SAT.

Plan and write an essay based on the following statement:

Now if I am to be no mere copper wire amateur but a luminous author, I must also be a most intensely refractory person, liable to go out and to go wrong at inconvenient moments, and with incendiary possibilities. These are the faults of my qualities; and I assure you that I sometimes dislike myself so much that when some irritable reviewer chances at that moment to pitch into me with zest, I feel unspeakably relieved and obliged.

–G. Bernard Shaw
from an "immoderately long letter"
to Arthur Bingham Walkley in 1903

Assignment: The above passage is from a letter that George Bernard Shaw submitted with his manuscript for *Man and Superman*. In an essay, explain why Shaw would feel "relieved and obliged" if his work were to endure harsh criticism. Support your explanation with evidence from your knowledge, classroom studies, experience and observation.

Thesis: Write a one-sentence response to the assignment. Make certain this single sentence offers a clear statement of your position.

Example: George Bernard Shaw knows that his own work is sometimes offensive or controversial, and it relieves him to hear that other people perceive it in that way—just as he planned.

Organizational Plan: If your thesis is the point on which you want to end, where does your essay need to begin? List the points of development that are inevitable in leading your reader from your beginning point to your end point. This list is your outline.

Draft: Use your thesis as both your beginning and your end. Following your outline, write a good first draft of your essay. Remember to support all your points with examples, facts, references to reading, etc.

Review and Revise: Exchange essays with a classmate. Using the Holistic scoring guide on page 225, score your partner's essay (while he or she scores yours). If necessary, rewrite your essay to correct the problems noted by your partner.

Identifying Sentence Errors

Identify the grammatical error in each of the following sentences. If the sentence contains no error, select answer choice E.

1. My oldest <u>sister, Marilyn</u> a talented <u>commercial artist,</u> <u>is also</u> a
              (A)   (B)   (C)
    <u>registered nurse.</u>   <u>No error</u>
         (D)   (E)

2. <u>Arguing with</u> a professor <u>in class</u> <u>will wreck havoc</u>
           (A)   (B)   (C)
    <u>with your grade.</u>   <u>No error</u>
          (D)   (E)

3. If the <u>repaired car</u> <u>were ready</u> to <u>be driven,</u> we <u>would of taken</u>
              (A)   (B)   (C)   (D)
    it home.   <u>No error</u>
                                      (E)

4. <u>The nurse</u> <u>suddenly jumps</u> <u>when the doctor</u> walked through the
       (A)   (B)   (C)
    door <u>to the operating room.</u>   <u>No error</u>
              (D)   (E)

5. I <u>do not like</u> <u>Shelly playing</u> the stereo <u>so loudly</u> <u>in the car.</u>
          (A)   (B)   (C)   (D)
    <u>No error</u>
        (E)

Improving Sentences

The underlined portion of each sentence below contains some flaw. Select the answer choice that best corrects the flaw.

6.   <u>I could watch the lake all day long playing computer solitaire is my only distraction.</u>
   A.   While I could watch the lake all day long and playing computer solitaire is my only distraction.
   B.   All day long playing computer solitaire is my only distraction when I could be watching the lake.
   C.   Playing computer solitaire all day long watching the lake is my only distraction.
   D.   My only distraction playing computer solitaire all day long watching the lake.
   E.   I could watch the lake all day long. Playing computer solitaire is my only distraction.

7.   Lisa was a girl who had to be in trouble before she would <u>turn the other cheek.</u>
   A.   get into a boat.
   B.   learn to float on her back.
   C.   back down.
   D.   make a stitch in time.
   E.   take a turn for the worse.

8.   <u>The dog was released by Stephanie and the guests were startled by the cheese platter when that was knocked on the floor by it.</u>
   A.   Stephanie released the dog and it startled the guests when the cheese platter was knocked onto the floor.
   B.   When Stephanie released the dog, it knocked the guests onto the floor with the cheese platter.
   C.   The dog startled Stephanie and the guests when, released, it knocked the cheese platter onto the floor.
   D.   Stephanie released the dog, and it startled the guests when it knocked the cheese platter onto the floor.
   E.   Stephanie released the dog and the guests were startled when it knocked the cheese platter onto the floor.

9. <u>Some teenagers were suspended for failing grades this year on Monday.</u>
   A. This year some teenagers were suspended for failing grades on Monday.
   B. On Monday, some teenagers were suspended for having failing grades this year.
   C. For failing grades Monday, some teenagers were suspended this year.
   D. Some teenagers this year for failing grades were suspended on Monday.
   E. Suspended for failing grades this year on Monday were some teenagers.

10. Henry bought a new computer that has a large memory <u>and having a DVD burner.</u>
    A. and a DVD burner.
    B. that has a DVD burner.
    C. for the DVD burner.
    D. and it has a DVD burner.
    E. with a DVD burner.

Lesson Ten

1. **fallible** (fal´ ə bəl) *adj.* capable of error
    All humans are *fallible* and sometimes make mistakes.
    syn: imperfect   *ant: infallible; flawless*

2. **blatant** (blāt´ nt) *adj.* obvious; too conspicuous
    His *blatant* efforts to get the girl's attention were embarrassing to every-
    one.
    syn: unconcealed; deliberate   *ant: secretive; cautious*

3. **dawdle** (dôd´ l) *v.* to waste time
    Bill, not wanting to go back to work, *dawdled* in the break room.
    syn: tarry; loiter   *ant: hasten; expedite*

4. **affiliate** (ə fil´ ē it) *n.* an associate; partner
    He denied that he was an *affiliate* of any organized-crime families.
    syn: member; colleague

5. **fawn** (fôn) *v.* to act slavishly submissive
    The young dancers *fawned* over the master of the ball and longed to be
    his partner.
    syn: grovel   *ant: ignore; disregard; neglect*

6. **calumny** (kal´ əm nē) *n.* a false and malicious accusation
    The candidate said that the accusation against him was a *calumny* meant
    to damage his reputation.
    syn: slander; slur   *ant: compliment*

7. **berate** (bi rāt´) *v.* to scold or rebuke severely and at length
    The coach *berated* the three players for arriving at the game late.
    syn: admonish; reprimand   *ant: praise*

8. **minion** (min´ yən) *n.* a fawning, servile follower
    The bully's *minions* obeyed him not out of loyalty, but out of fear.
    syn: lackey   *ant: leader*

9. **desolate** (des´ ə lit) *adj.* lonely; forlorn; uninhabited; barren
    The castaway spent four years on a *desolate* island, many miles from the
    mainland.
    syn: deserted; bleak   *ant: populous; cheerful*

10. **bane** (bān) *n.* the cause of ruin, harm, distress, or death
The *bane* of the defeated alien invaders turned out to be the common cold.
syn: blight; curse   *ant: aid; assistance*

11. **pacify** (pas´ ə fī) *v.* to calm down
Grandmother was able to *pacify* the irritable baby.
syn: appease; placate   *ant: provoke; agitate*

12. **garble** (gär´ bəl) *v.* to mix up or distort
Jill's speech would have been good if she had not *garbled* the facts.
syn: jumble; corrupt

13. **prevaricate** (pri vâr´ i kāt) *v.* to lie
When asked about the crime, Jim *prevaricated* because he did not want to incriminate his friend.
syn: hedge

14. **filch** (filch) *v.* to steal
The woman *filched* my purse when I left the room to answer the telephone.
syn: pilfer; pinch

15. **neophyte** (nē´ ə fīt) *n.* a beginner
Though Sara was a *neophyte* at golf, she outplayed most of the veterans.
syn: novice; amateur   *ant: expert; veteran*

EXERCISE I—Words in Context

From the list below, supply the words needed to complete the paragraph. Some words will not be used.

calumny	dawdle	minion	garble
bane	affiliate	prevaricate	

1. To avoid prosecution, the crime boss relied on his _____ to do his dirty work for him. The _____ of the organization knew that if they were arrested, they took the fall alone; however, the boss's overconfidence in his associates proved to be his _____ when Knox, a hit man, testified against him in court. The boss claimed, of course, that the testimony was merely a spiteful _____ designed to embarrass him; however, the boss could not _____ cleverly enough to convince the jury that he was innocent.

From the list below, supply the words needed to complete the paragraph. Some words will not be used.

dawdle	minion	berate	blatant
filch	fawn	pacify	

2. Gina couldn't stand her friend's _____ attempt to get Lonnie to ask her to the dance. For weeks, Jamie _____ over Lonnie, even though he barely recognized her when they passed in the hall. Occasionally, Gina _____ her friend for being so foolish.

    "Don't _____ by waiting for him," Gina would say. "The dance is tomorrow; ask someone you actually know." Jamie usually got angry when Gina lectured her.

    "Will you leave me alone, please?" Gina often replied. "I'm almost ready to take my dog to the dance just to _____ your nagging."

From the list below, supply the words needed to complete the paragraph. Some words will not be used.

neophyte	bane	fallible	filch
garble	desolate	prevaricate	

3. "Even the most experienced hikers are _____ in climates as harsh as this one," said the desert guide as he turned and squinted at the miles of _____ sand dunes that stretched to the horizon. "If there's one message that I can't _____, it's to bring plenty of water. You _____ who haven't hiked in the desert before will soon learn that once you're out there in the dunes, water is nonexistent. What you manage to _____ from the various plants or from beneath the ground will not be enough to sustain you."

EXERCISE II—Sentence Completion

Complete the sentence in a way that shows you understand the meaning of the italicized vocabulary word.

1.   *Affiliates* of the organization were invited to...

2.   Craig *garbles* his speech when...

3.   I'm just a *neophyte* at this card game, so please...

4.   In a small town, spreading *calumny* about someone could...

5.   That sports car is bound to be your *bane* if you continue to...

6.   The *desolate* barn was the perfect place for...

7.   If you *dawdle* all night, you won't...

8.   The cab driver *berated* the pedestrian who...

9.   Nicole learned that even computers can be *fallible* when she...

10.   Some of the fans at the concert *fawned* over...

11.   The pickpocket must have *filched* my wallet when he...

12.   When asked by his wife how the new dress fit, Randy *prevaricated* because he thought...

13.   Neil was asked to leave the restaurant after his *blatant* attempt to...

14.   The crooked government official was never arrested because it was his *minions* who...

15.   Jennie had to *pacify* her dog after it...

EXERCISE III—Roots, Prefixes, and Suffixes

Study the entries and answer the questions that follow.

The roots *corp* and *corpor* mean "body."
The root *rupt* means "to break."
The prefix *inter* means "between" or "among."

1. *Using literal translations as guidance, define the following words without using a dictionary.*

    A. corporal   D. interrupt
    B. corporation   E. erupt
    C. incorporate   F. corrupt

2. If someone's appendix *ruptures*, then it _____. If a bank has no money, then it can be described as _____.

3. List as many words as you can think of that contain the roots *corp*, *rupt*, or the prefix *inter*.

EXERCISE IV—Inference

Complete the sentences by inferring information about the italicized word from its context.

1. If you *dawdle* too long before leaving for the airport, you might...

2. Since Ben's answering machine *garbled* the incoming message, Ben did not...

3. If police are trying to *pacify* the crowd, then people in the crowd must be...

EXERCISE V—Critical Reading

Below is a reading passage followed by several multiple-choice questions similar to the ones you will encounter on the SAT. Carefully read the passage and choose the best answer for each of the questions.

The following passage describes a couple who have not allowed sightlessness to impede their energetic lifestyle.

1   There is one style of golf that professionals have yet to experience. The style is to shut the eyes tightly, tee up, and then drive the little white ball toward the first hole. Who but a sightless person could imagine playing golf that way on every outing? Is there anything more unbelievable than trying to play golf without being able to see the club, the ball, the tee, and the course?

2   At least two golfers, Mary and Joe, always play golf that way. Mary and Joe were born blind; they have never had the luxury of seeing where their drives land—on the course or off.

3   The couple recently spent time with friends in the country, and after a few days of lawn parties, shopping trips, dining out, and neighborhood strolling, the foursome went golfing at a college course where Mary and Joe were reportedly the first blind people to golf.

4   According to Joe, golf is something different to do. It is a good form of outdoor recreation and exercise. He took up golf a few years ago when he began to have a little free time, and surprisingly, golf is fairly tame compared to the couple's other endeavors, such as canoeing and downhill skiing. Mary enjoys the summer outdoor activity as much as her winter bowling league, which she joined to alleviate the boredom that cold weather brings to outdoor types.

5   Joe says his long game of golf is better than his short; Mary, however, putts as close to the mark as any golfer. Her ball frequently rolls to within one or two feet from the pin after thirty-foot putts on the green.

6   Learning to play golf is not much different for the blind than the sighted, says Joe, and the clubs are exactly the same. Coaches who accompany Mary and Joe on golf outings have had their techniques handed down from past trainers of the blind, and the only extra guidance the players get is a verbal point in the right direction before they hit. Rules and regulations remain the same as for sighted golfers; there are no gimmies just because a player literally can't see the lie before the shot. For practice, Mary and Joe go to driving and putting ranges. There, a coach sets up the shots and positions the golfers so that they hit the ball when they swing. The golfers then work on perfecting their swings and directing their shots. They strive for consistency and good contact with the ball, listening for that great sound that every golfer longs to hear when the club smacks the ball just right. Mary and Joe are in their second year on the links, and they have graduated from playing nine-hole games to playing eighteen-hole games.

7   Navigation on a golf course, in a bowling alley, or behind a boat pulling them on water skis (where they say they can hear the wake on each side of them), is no big deal for this athletic pair; in fact, they are at a point in which their own guide dogs cannot always accompany them on their adventures.

When Mary and Joe hit the slopes, the guide dogs must stay home because of the potential danger to other skiers. Dogs are not welcome on golf courses or tennis courts, either.

8   While Mary and Joe love sports, they also have, between the two of them, over forty years of high-level office experience. With assistance from the guide dogs, Mary and Joe use foot power and public transportation to navigate from the suburbs to their offices in the bustling city.

9   The couple has many other outside interests, including membership in advocacy organizations, sports leagues, religious affiliations, and volunteer networks. They are not unaware of the many so-called comical remarks of sighted people about those without vision, but they often lead the conversation by making fun of themselves. Mary and Joe are down-to-earth people who have never asked any favors because of their blindness, and they do not expect to be treated any differently than anyone else.

10   In the unique setting of a golf course, it is unusual to watch a blind couple enjoying such a precise sport. It is more unusual to consider that in the short time that they have been playing, Mary and Joe have better golf games than many of their sighted friends have. One must imagine how their friends feel.

1.   According to the passage, how did Mary and Joe lose their sight?
      A. Joe was born blind, and Mary went blind in childhood.
      B. When they were both ten, a disease took their sight.
      C. They were both born blind.
      D. Mary is partially sighted, and Joe went blind during college.
      E. Joe lost an eye while golfing, and Mary was born blind.

2.   According to paragraph 4, Joe took up golf when
      A. he had free time.
      B. he needed exercise.
      C. he wanted outdoor recreation.
      D. he wanted something tame.
      E. he wanted to compete with Mary

3.   Joe has a good long game, but Mary has a better
      A. drive.
      B. chip.
      C. swing.
      D. short game.
      E. trouble slice.

4. According to paragraph 6, the main difference between golf for sighted people and golf for blind people is
    A. the length of the clubs.
    B. the size of the putting clubs.
    C. the use of verbal directions.
    D. the rules and regulations.
    E. the gimmies.

5. As used in paragraph 6, *lie* most nearly means
    A. an untruth.
    B. the flight of the ball.
    C. the guide dog.
    D. the position of the ball.
    E. the coach.

6. During practice, which of the following indicates to Mary and Joe that they are hitting well?
    A. the sound of a well-hit ball
    B. consistency
    C. eighteen-hole golf courses
    D. the feel of the swing
    E. the number of years that they have been playing

7. How do Mary and Joe manage to get to their places of employment?
    A. by taxi and scooter
    B. by bus and train
    C. by public transportation and walking
    D. by hitchhiking and train
    E. by guide dog and taxi

8. How do Mary and Joe handle jokes about blindness?
    A. They ignore them.
    B. They reprimand the joke tellers.
    C. They secretly scorn the joke tellers.
    D. They walk away angry.
    E. They make fun of themselves.

9. Which could you infer from the following sentences?

    It is more unusual to consider that in the short time that they have been playing, Mary and Joe have better golf games than many of their sighted friends. One must imagine how their friends feel.

    A. Friends might be chagrined if they lose at golf to Mary and Joe.
    B. Friends take advantage of Mary and Joe.
    C. Mary and Joe have blind friends.
    D. The friends like to golf with Mary and Joe.
    E. Mary and Joe like to ski with their friends.

10. Which of the following statements best identifies the point of the article?
    A. Golf is a good game.
    B. Optimism is a type of game.
    C. Blind people play golf with their eyes closed.
    D. Anything is possible with diligent effort.
    E. Playing golf is possible for sightless people.

11. Of the following types of publications, which would be most likely to publish this article?
    A. country home and garden magazine
    B. skiing magazine
    C. instruction brochure
    D. local newspaper column
    E. book about golf techniques

Lesson Eleven

1. **flagrant** (flā´ grənt) *adj.* glaringly bad; outrageous
His *flagrant* disregard for authority caused the boy a lot of trouble.
syn: offensive; shameless; brazen

2. **patrician** (pə trish´ ən) *n.* an aristocrat
The *patrician* could not marry the man she loved, because he was a member of the working class.
syn: noble   *ant: commoner*

3. **emissary** (em´ i ser ē) *n.* one sent on a special mission to represent others
Before the concept of diplomatic immunity, an *emissary* was often imprisoned or killed.
syn: ambassador; agent

4. **kindred** (kin´ drid) *adj.* having similar origin, nature, or character
They had met only days ago, but the two girls were *kindred* spirits and immediately became friends.
syn: homogeneous   *ant: disparate*

5. **fracas** (frā´ kəs) *n.* a loud quarrel or fight
The coaches broke up the *fracas* that began on the playing field during the game.
syn: brawl

6. **lacerate** (las´ ə rāt) *v.* to tear (flesh) jaggedly
The pedal *lacerated* the rider's leg when the bicycle flipped over.
syn: slash; gash; rip   *ant: suture*

7. **futile** (fyōōt´ 1) *adj.* useless; pointless
I received a shock during my *futile* attempt to fix the television set.
syn: ineffectual; fruitless   *ant: effective; useful*

8. **immaculate** (im mak´ yə lit) *adj.* spotless; perfect
The rooms of the mansion were as *immaculate* as the grounds surrounding the large estate.
syn: clean; pure   *ant: dirty; soiled; spotted*

9. **gait** (gāt) *n.* manner of walking
The horse's smooth *gait* made riding easy.
syn: walk

10. **carp** (kärp) *v.* to complain or to find fault in a petty or nagging way
No one wants to talk to you because you *carp* about every little thing.
syn: grumble; nag; nitpick   *ant: praise; laud*

11. **query** (kwēr´ ē) *v.* to ask; inquire
The buyer decided to *query* the previous owners about the leaky plumbing before buying the house.
syn: question; interrogate

12. **queue** (kyōō) *n.* a line of people or vehicles
During the war, *queues* formed in front of butcher shops because meat was in short supply.

13. **nefarious** (nə fâr´ ē əs) *adj.* very wicked; notorious
Billy the Kid was one of the most *nefarious* characters of the Old West.
syn: villainous; despicable   *ant: reputable; honest*

14. **genesis** (jen´ ə sis) *n.* beginning; origin
The invention of the telegraph marked the *genesis* of the Information Age.
syn: start; birth   *ant: conclusion; finish*

15. **facade** (fə säd´) *n.* a deceptive outward appearance;
        a misrepresentation
Joan's cheerful *facade* did not hide her depression.
syn: pretense; charade

EXERCISE I—Words in Context

From the list below, supply the words needed to complete the paragraph. Some words will not be used.

gait	futile	kindred	immaculate
emissary	query	nefarious	facade

1. When Cal took a job working at the docks, he didn't realize that he was going to become a[n] _____ for a[n] _____ businessman who made a fortune shipping black-market goods. After one week of unloading crates from ships and putting them on trucks during the graveyard shift, Cal _____ the supervisor as to the contents of the heavy wood boxes. The question was _____; the supervisor just looked at Cal, paused for an uneasy moment, and then replied, "Tractor parts." At that moment, Cal realized that he was participating in a[n] _____ that concealed some type of illegal operation; even worse, he was a pawn for the business-man—if U.S. Customs were to raid the dock, Cal would probably be arrest-ed while the boss's record remained _____.

From the list below, supply the words needed to complete the paragraph. Some words will not be used.

genesis	emissary	gait
queue	patrician	carp

2. After six hours of driving, Charlie parked his car and walked across the parking lot with an odd _____. He was happy to stretch his legs, but he _____ about summer crowds when he saw that the _____ for the restroom extended around the corner of the rest stop. He should have expected as much, he reasoned; Memorial Day weekend was the annual _____ of the summer season. With the summer season, of course, come summer crowds.

From the list below, supply the words needed to complete the paragraph. Some words will not be used.

flagrant	immaculate	lacerate	fracas
patrician	kindred	nefarious	

3. Most of the servants abandoned the grounds when they heard the
    _____ outside the front gates. A crowd of armed peasants gathered
    below, preparing to punish their _____ for what they described as
    a[n] _____ abuse of his title. Disease and famine were rampant
    throughout the villages of the manor, but Lord Geoffrey continued to raise
    taxes and host feasts for his _____ aristocrats. Nervously, Geoffrey
    peered from his chamber window to see his guards surrendering to the
    mob. The angry farmers and merchants did not _____ the guards
    with their pitchforks and poorly fashioned swords, but Geoffrey knew that
    they would not be so merciful with him. In a fit of panic, he began think-
    ing of possible escape routes as the mob flooded into the courtyard through
    the gate.

EXERCISE II—Sentence Completion

Complete the sentence in a way that shows you understand the meaning of the italicized vocabulary word.

1.   A *fracas* developed in the parking lot after...

2.   Every day during work, the customer service representative had to listen to people *carp* about...

3.   In American culture, it is *flagrant* disrespect to...

4.   The largely outnumbered army built hundreds of fires at night to create a *facade* that...

5.   The *queue* at the ticket window was so long that Kim decided to...

6.   The broken glass on the floor will *lacerate* your feet if you do not...

7.   You should *query* the post office about the package if...

8.   The officer suspected that something *nefarious* was occurring in the bank when he saw...

9.   The photograph in the guide showed an *immaculate* park area, but the real park was...

10. Before the *genesis* of the age of automobiles, people relied on...

11. The affluent *patrician* knew that his family would frown upon him for...

12. Despite their *kindred* roots, the two brothers...

13. Serena knew that if she didn't approach the podium with a confident *gait*, the audience would...

14. The United Nations sent an *emissary* to the poverty-stricken nation to...

15. Efforts to contain the floodwaters proved *futile* when...

EXERCISE III—Roots, Prefixes, and Suffixes

Study the entries and answer the questions that follow.

The root *am* means "friend" or "to love."
The root *aqu* means "water."
The root *brev* means "short."
The root *prot* means "first" or "original."

1. *Using literal translations as guidance, define the following words without using a dictionary.*

    A. amicable   D. aquatic
    B. amative   E. prototype
    C. aquarium   F. protagonist

2. If a word is long and you don't want to write it out, you might simply use its _____. If a speaker is known for her *brevity*, then her speeches must be _____.

3. Someone in a loving mood might be described as being _____. That person might be in love with, or _____ of, someone else.

4. List as many words as you can think of that contain the roots *aqu* or *prot*.

EXERCISE IV—Inference

Complete the sentences by inferring information about the italicized word from its context.

1. If you *carp* about the decorations in your friend's new home, then your friend might not...

2. A criminal who is imprisoned for *nefarious* crimes must have done things that...

3. If a particular approach to solving a problem seems *futile*, then you should...

EXERCISE V—Writing

Here is a writing prompt similar to the one you will find on the writing portion of the SAT.

Plan and write an essay based on the following statement:

The farther backward you can look, the farther forward you are likely to see.

–Sir Winston Churchill

Assignment: In an essay, rephrase Churchill's statement in your own words and explain whether you agree or disagree with it. Does the assertion apply to all humanity or only individuals? Does it apply to the present time, or just certain periods in history? Support your essay with evidence from your own reading, classroom studies, experiences and observations.

Thesis: Write a one-sentence response to the assignment. Make certain this single sentence offers a clear statement of your position.

Example: According to Sir Winston Churchill, history repeats itself, and a good memory is the best tool for predicting the future.

Organizational Plan: If your thesis is the point on which you want to end, where does your essay need to begin? List the points of development that are inevitable in leading your reader from your beginning point to your end point. This list is your outline.

Draft: Use your thesis as both your beginning and your end. Following your outline, write a good first draft of your essay. Remember to support all your points with examples, facts, references to reading, etc.

Review and Revise: Exchange essays with a classmate. Using the scoring guide for Organization on page 221, score your partner's essay (while he or she scores yours). Focus on the organizational plan and use of language conventions. If necessary, rewrite your essay to improve the organizational plan and/or your use of language.

Improving Paragraphs

Read the following passage and then answer the multiple-choice questions that fol-
low. The questions will require you to make decisions regarding the revision of the
reading selection.

(1) While riding on a roller coaster moving seventy miles per hour, you probably need to squint your eyes to see, or they well up with tears. (2) Your hair and
your shirt flap in the wind like streamers, and your hat, if you wore one, have long
departed.

(3) Now imagine that you are in freefall, 5000 feet above the surface of the earth,
and you have just reached a terminal velocity of 120 miles per hour. (4) Seeing anything without goggles is impossible, and the material of your jumpsuit flaps so
quickly that it makes a buzzing sound. (5) Now picture yourself in the cockpit of a
fighter jet that's plummeting toward earth at 800 miles per hour, faster than sound,
and faster than some bullets. (6) You're at 10,000 feet, and the aircraft is out of control. (7) If you stay with the plane, you will die in seconds. (8) If you eject, you
might be killed instantly. (9) Unimaginable? (10) Not for Captain Brian Udell.

(11) During a nighttime Air Force training sortie off the coast of North Carolina,
the instruments in Captain Udell's F-15E Strike Eagle malfunctioned. (12) One set
told him everything was fine, while the other suggested a pending disaster. (13) The
heads-up display indicated that his flight status was normal, but, according to other
(functioning) indicators, his jet was plummeting straight to earth at nearly supersonic speed. (14) In little more than a second, Udell gave Dennis White, the
weapons system officer, the order to bail out, and by the time the canopy blew at
5,000 feet, the jet had accelerated to over 780 miles per hour—1,200 feet per
second.

(15) Udell's ACES II ejection seat cleared the aircraft at 3,000 feet above the
ocean. (16) Air resistance at mach 1 shredded Udell as he slowed to subsonic
speeds, but luckily, his chute functioned and caught the air at less than 1,000 feet,
had he hesitated just one half-second longer, the chute would not have deployed in
time, and the impact on the water would have killed him.

(17) Don't ask Udell what is was like to travel at mach 1 without the luxury of
a plane; he is glad to have no memory of the three seconds that followed the pull of
the ejection lever. (18) He only recollects his descent to the water, pulling his broken body into a waterlogged raft and then discovering how the ejection had bat-
tered his body. (19) His mask and helmet had been stripped from his head, and anything he had in his pockets had torn through. (20) His flight suit was shredded, and
the skin of his face was stretched and swollen. (21) His arm and ankle were dislo-
cated, his rib was cracked, and the tendons in his right knee were so damaged that
his lower leg flopped uselessly onto his other leg when he flipped it into the raft.
(22) The injuries were substantial, but the price was relatively small; Captain
White, the weapons officer, did not survive the ejection. (23) Udell waited alone,
cold and broken in the dark water, for four hours before the Coast Guard located
him. (24) Two months and several surgeries after the unfortunate night, Brian Udell
walked again. (25) Eight months later, Udell was back in the cockpit, but the lifelong pilot (he learned to fly when he was nine), had a different perspective of his
aviation career: it would always be second to the family he almost left behind.

1. Which of the following suggestions corrects the error in sentence 2?
   A. Replace *you* with *one would.*
   B. Replace *have* with *has.*
   C. Replace *flap* with *flaps.*
   D. Form two sentences from sentence 1.
   E. Combine both sentences.

2. Which of the following changes to paragraph 2 would improve the flow of the passage?
   A. Delete *Unimaginable.*
   B. Combine sentences 3 and 4.
   C. Insert a comma after *flaps.*
   D. Begin a new paragraph after sentence 2.
   E. Replace *You're* with *your.*

3. Which unnecessary sentence should be deleted from paragraph 3?
   A. Sentence 11
   B. Sentence 12
   C. Sentence 13
   D. Sentence 14
   E. Sentences 11 and 14

4. Which suggestion would correct a grammatical error in paragraph 4?
   A. Put a period after *1000 feet* and capitalize *had.*
   B. Change *ACES* to lowercase letters.
   C. Replace *killed* with *hurt.*
   D. Combine sentences 15 and 16.
   E. Combine paragraphs 4 and 5.

5. What would best conclude the passage?
   A. Replace the semicolon after *small* with a period.
   B. In one more paragraph, compare Udell's experience to an automobile race.
   C. Include a paragraph about Udell's family.
   D. Begin a new paragraph after *pockets tore through.*
   E. Begin a new paragraph after *Coast Guard located him.*

Lesson Twelve

1. **deluge** (del´ yōōj) *n.* a flood; an overwhelming rush
    The new amusement park experienced a *deluge* of visitors on opening day.
    syn: inundation; surge   *ant: drought; dearth*

2. **catholic** (kath´ ə lik) *adj.* universal; wide-ranging
    His *catholic* interests made him quite knowledgeable in many subjects.
    syn: broad   *ant: provincial; limited; parochial*

3. **eerie** (ēr´ ē) *adj.* weird; mysterious; strange and frightening
    No one accepted the dare to stay in the *eerie* old mansion for one night.
    syn: creepy; sinister   *ant: common; ordinary*

4. **martial** (mär´ shəl) *adj.* warlike; relating to the military
    A state of *martial* law was declared in the small country in the weeks following the overthrow of the government.

5. **anthropomorphic** (an´ thrə pə môr´ fik) *adj.* attributing human characteristics or qualities to objects, animals, or gods
    Anthropomorphic stories might feature pigs and rabbits walking upright, wearing clothes, and speaking to each other in human languages.

6. **beneficiary** (ben ə fish´ ē er ē) *n.* one who receives benefits
    John was the sole *beneficiary* of his Uncle Martin's vast estate.
    syn: recipient; heir

7. **careen** (kə rēn´) *v.* to swerve or lurch from side to side while in motion
    The torrential winds caused the ship to *careen* violently.
    syn: tilt

8. **aplomb** (ə plum´) *n.* self-confidence
    The *aplomb* of the young dancer astonished the veterans of the troupe.
    syn: assurance; poise   *ant: awkwardness*

9. **guile** (gīl) *n.* slyness and cunning in dealing with others
    Brad's *guile* contributed to his wealth, but it also created enemies.
    syn: craftiness; astuteness   *ant: honesty*

10. **modicum** (mod´ i kəm) *n.* a small amount
    A sudden shower gave us a *modicum* of relief from the heat and humidity.
    syn: bit   *ant: abundance*

11. **fester** (fes´ tər) *v.* to grow embittered over time; to rot
    If allowed to *fester,* dislike can turn into bitter hatred.
    syn: aggravate; worsen

12. **languish** (lang´ gwish) *v.* to become weak or feeble; to lose strength
    I *languished* at the thought of all the work that still needed to be done.
    syn: wither; fade   *ant: thrive*

13. **pall** (pôl) *n.* something that covers or conceals
    A *pall* of gloom descended over the crowd.
    syn: shroud

14. **havoc** (hav´ ək) *n.* great destruction; chaos
    The commandos wreaked *havoc* throughout the area when they
    infiltrated the secret base.
    syn: mayhem; disorder   *ant: order*

15. **rancid** (ran´ sid) *adj.* having a bad taste or smell; spoiled
    The bitter fight over child custody left a *rancid* taste in both lawyers'
    mouths.
    syn: rotten; repulsive   *ant: fresh*

EXERCISE I—Words in Context

*From the list below, supply the words needed to complete the paragraph. Some
words will not be used.*

deluge	pall	careen	fester
modicum	martial	beneficiary	

1. Everyone anticipated the opening of the new state park, but not the strict,
   almost _____ rules and prohibitions that imposed fines for camping,
   cooking, swimming, or walking in unauthorized areas. Immediately after
   the park opened, the Department of Parks and Recreation received a[n]
   _____ of letters questioning who, exactly, the _____ of the new
   park were supposed to be, since the people who paid for the park apparently were not. Without at least a[n] _____ of freedom to explore the
   old forest, people complained, the park was simply private property. Most
   agreed that the park would be wonderful without the _____ of
   restrictions hanging over it.

From the list below, supply the words needed to complete the paragraph. Some words will not be used.

fester	aplomb	**guile**	havoc
languish	rancid	pall	

2. The power outage brought _____ to the meat processing plant. For hours, workers _____ in the dark struggling to move tons of perishable food to refrigerated trailers before it began to _____ in the rapidly warming warehouse. Any meat left in the facility after a designated time was declared _____ and marked for disposal. Many workers worried about the fate of the company, but the owner reassured them and asked them with _____ to keep their composure through the crisis.

From the list below, supply the words needed to complete the paragraph. Some words will not be used.

catholic	eerie	**martial**	careen
guile	rancid	anthropomorphic	

3. The children's book features _____ animal characters that speak and interact as though they were people. In the story, a sneaky wolf uses his _____ to manipulate a chicken into leaving its pen and entering the _____ old forest behind the farm. The wolf, of course, then tries to eat the chicken, but the chicken _____ around rocks and trees, causing the wolf to become dizzy and give up the chase. Like many children's books, this one has _____ themes that appeal to all audiences.

EXERCISE II—Sentence Completion

Complete the sentence in a way that shows you understand the meaning of the italicized vocabulary word.

1. The youth camp is designed to build up the *aplomb* of children by...

2. Eric expected to find *eerie* paintings hanging on the walls when he...

3. You'll *languish* early in the race if you...

4. She knew that the milk was *rancid* because...

5. The producers wanted the new sitcom to be *catholic* enough to appeal to...

6. Renee has the *guile* to become...

7. Sandy thought the rules in her new school seemed almost *martial* because...

9. Randy wanted only a *modicum* of silence after a long day of...

10. A *deluge* of customers swamped the store on the day that...

11. Tim was Howard's *beneficiary*, so when Howard died, Tim...

12. The potato salad will *fester* in the sun, so you should...

13. Foods that wreak *havoc* on your teeth include...

14. The smog created a *pall* that...

15. The car *careened* all over the highway when the driver...

EXERCISE III—Roots, Prefixes, and Suffixes

Study the entries and answer the questions that follow.

The roots *patr* and *patern* mean "father."
The root *scop* means "to watch."
The roots *scrib* and *script* mean "to write."
The root *cent* means "one hundred."

1. Using literal translations as guidance, define the following words without using a dictionary.

    A. manuscript D. centennial
    B. scripture   E. percent
    C. scribe   F. horoscope

2. To see things far away, you might watch them through a[n] _____, but to see tiny things, might use a[n] _____.

3. *Arch* means "ruler," so a male leader of a family is called a[n] _____. If you talk down to someone as though you were the father and he were the child, you are said to _____ that person. A _____ test can verify that someone is the father of a child.

4. List as many words as you can think of that contain the roots *scrib* or *script*.

EXERCISE IV—Inference

Complete the sentences by inferring information about the italicized word from its context.

1. You are the *beneficiary* on my insurance policy, so if anything happens to me, you will…

2. *Anthropomorphic* animals in literature might speak English, drive cars, or do anything that makes them…

3. Only a *modicum* of readers claimed to dislike the…

EXERCISE V—Critical Reading

Below is a pair of reading passages followed by several multiple-choice questions similar to the ones you will encounter on the SAT. Carefully read both passages and choose the best answer to each of the questions.

The following passages discuss parts of women's suffrage. The first passage focuses on famous suffragettes. The second passage describes barriers that the suffragettes had to overcome.

Passage 1

Women have been fighting for equal rights since the middle of the nineteenth century. While some women argue that they still do not have equal rights, they cannot argue that the cause has come a long way since Elizabeth Cady Stanton and Susan B. Anthony took the first steps toward the acceptance of
5 women's suffrage.

Elizabeth Cady Stanton was a pioneer for women's rights before her time. At her own wedding, she appalled her guests by intentionally omitting the word "obey" while reciting her vows; fortunately, her husband supported her views that women were equal to men. Driven by her cause, Stanton—a mother of seven
10 children—made time to become a leading activist for the rights of women. She wrote speeches for Susan B. Anthony, she spoke at numerous women's rights conventions, and, using the Declaration of Independence for inspiration, she drafted the 1848 Seneca Falls declaration. New Englanders were familiar with the powerful rhetoric in her speeches. She believed that women were morally supe-
15 rior and therefore deserved the right to participate in politics.

Susan B. Anthony, born in Massachusetts, was also a pioneer in the women's rights arena. While a young schoolgirl, Anthony questioned her teacher as to why he only taught long division to boys. He explained that women did not need to know how to do long division—only how to read a Bible and run a home.
20 Anthony then took it upon herself to learn long division by listening in on the teacher's long division lessons to the boys. Anthony became so prominent as a women's rights advocate that women who joined the cause were called "Susie Bs." One of Anthony's defining moments came when she, along with a few other women, registered to vote during the election of 1871. Fifteen women actually
25 succeeded in voting, and though they were later arrested and fined, they did not fail in making history.

If it were not for these forerunners who took the first arduous steps toward equal rights, women's rights would be nowhere near where they are today. These difficult strides have secured a nation in which women are free to earn a living,
30 govern states, or run for president. Elizabeth Cady Stanton and Susan B. Anthony deserve the thanks for over a century of progress, and many women look to them as role models and inspiration.

Passage 2

Many who are aware of the women's suffrage movement are not aware of the depths of the opposition that tried to quash the effort. Many wise, brave women worked hard in the quest for rights, but there were even more men who fought against them. The anti-suffragists maintained several reasons for their resistance,
5 from questions of morality to the physical limitations of women. In the present, most of the reasons would be dismissed as silly, but in the nineteenth century, they were considerable roadblocks to women's suffrage.

Physical limitations of women was a significant part of the anti-suffragist platform, and some men still, to this day, consider it to be legitimate. Women,
10 according to men in the nineteenth century, lacked the capacity to make important decisions or even the physical stamina to actually make the decisions. A number of men proposed that women would be so physically exhausted by making the trip to the poll that they would be too disoriented to make intelligent choices! A woman's emotional instability, the men also argued, affected women's
15 ability to reason, thus disqualifying them from voting.

Some challengers claimed that it would have been immoral to allow women to vote. Drawing on the Bible's Genesis, some men maintained the theory that once Eve gained wisdom from the tree of knowledge, everything went downhill; if women were to get what they wanted—voting rights—everything would go
20 downhill again. Other men suggested that women who wore long sleeves would be compelled to cheat by concealing extra ballots and voting more than once; apparently, it never occurred to the men that they were able to do the same thing when they wore long sleeves!

Perhaps the most shocking anti-suffragist tactic was to describe women's suf-
25 frage as a harbinger to the destruction of the traditional family structure. They warned that women would lose their feminine qualities if they assumed male responsibilities such as voting. In reaction to the shifting gender roles, men would become effeminate. Once these roles were corrupted, the entire family structure would suffer and eventually fall apart.

30 Most of the anti-suffragist arguments lacked any plausible evidence to support them; they were simply cries of desperation in the face of great changes in the world. Some of the other prophecies have been realized, but through the decades, society has come to understand them not as negative consequences, necessarily, but as products of an advancing civilization. Gender roles have
35 indeed changed since the birth of the women's rights movement, and the traditional family structure is also changing. Women's suffrage was, without a doubt, a crucial step in human progress, but like any great change, it had advocates and adversaries.

1. The purpose of passage 1 is to
   A. inform.
   B. persuade.
   C. entertain.
   D. challenge.
   E. laud.

2. Which of the following is *not* a way that Stanton, as a leading activist, helped the cause of women's suffrage?
   A. leaving out "obey" from wedding vows
   B. writing speeches for Anthony
   C. drafting the Seneca Falls declaration
   D. speaking at women's rights conventions
   E. her powerful rhetoric

3. As used in line 14 of the first passage, *rhetoric* most nearly means
   A. speaking.
   B. style of speaking.
   C. the study of principles and rules of composition.
   D. knowledge.
   E. a type of language.

4. Which of the following is evidence of Anthony's widespread influence?
   A. She taught herself long division.
   B. Women who followed her were called "Suzy Bs."
   C. She registered to vote.
   D. Fifteen women voted.
   E. She was able to cast a ballot.

5. In line 9 of second passage, *platform* means
   A. theater stage.
   B. declaration of principles.
   C. point of view.
   D. place to speak.
   E. common ground.

6. According to the second passage, which was *not* a potential effect on family life if women were granted suffrage?
   A. Women would assume male responsibilities.
   B. Women would lose their feminine qualities.
   C. Masculinity would become obsolete.
   D. Men would become effeminate.
   E. The family structure would fall apart.

7. As used in line 25 of the second passage, *harbinger* most nearly means
   A. an attack.
   B. an omen.
   C. a result.
   D. a deletion.
   E. a message.

8. Which of the following is a product of an advancing civilization, according to the second passage?
   A. Women cheat by voting twice.
   B. Traditional family roles change.
   C. Women grow emotionally stable.
   D. People vote electronically.
   E. Men cease voting.

9. The overall tone of passage 2 is
   A. severely critical.
   B. speculative.
   C. mildly ironic.
   D. apathetic.
   E. condemning.

10. The authors of both passages would probably agree that
    A. women have no place in politics.
    B. individuals can make more of a difference than groups.
    C. some women earned the right to vote, but others do not deserve it.
    D. the right to vote is precious.
    E. gender roles will always be different for men and women.

11. Both passages portray the women's suffrage movement as
    A. positive and necessary.
    B. arduous and ongoing.
    C. senseless and futile.
    D. risky and luck-driven.
    E. historic and ineffective.

Lesson Thirteen

1. **holocaust** (hol´ ə kôst) *n.* a great or complete destruction of life
Many feared that the Cuban Missile Crisis was going to end in a nuclear *holocaust.*

2. **embroil** (em broil´) *v.* to draw into a conflict or fight
The new zoning ordinance *embroiled* members of the planning committee.
syn: entangle

3. **anachronism** (a nak´ rə niz əm) *n.* something or someone existing outside of its proper time
Some consider the use of fossil fuels to be an *anachronism* in this age of nuclear technology.

4. **denigrate** (den´ i grāt) *v.* to attack the reputation of; to speak ill of
The senator, who opposed political mudslinging, refused to *denigrate* his opponent.
syn: defame; belittle   *ant: praise; promote*

5. **humane** (hyōō mān´) *adj.* kind; compassionate
Putting the critically injured horse out of its misery is the most *humane* course of action.
syn: kindly; benevolent; considerate   *ant: inhumane; cruel*

6. **effusive** (i fyōō´ siv) *adj.* emotionally excessive; overly demonstrative
I don't argue with you in public because your *effusive* responses embarrass me.
syn: gushing   *ant: reserved; restrained*

7. **defunct** (di fungkt´) *adj.* no longer in existence
Don't get scammed into buying stock in a *defunct* corporation.
syn: invalid; extinct

8. **lackey** (lak´ ē) *n.* a slavish follower
I want to speak to the boss, not a *lackey* who screens visitors for him.
syn: minion

9. **envisage** (en viz´ ij) *v.* to form a mental picture
You should *envisage* the task before you begin it.
syn: imagine; visualize

10. **lament** (lə ment´) *v.* to mourn
    Devoted fans *lamented* the death of the popular singer.
    syn: grieve   *ant: rejoice*

11. **gape** (gāp) *v.* to stare with an open mouth
    The child *gaped* at his mother in astonishment when she switched off the television.

12. **impertinent** (im pûr´ tn ənt) *adj.* rude and disrespectful
    The boy earned an after-school detention for his *impertinent* behavior.
    syn: insolent; impolite   *ant: polite; courteous*

13. **haughty** (hô´ tē) *adj.* arrogant; proud
    The poorly dressed visitor drew a *haughty* look from the butler.
    syn: arrogant   *ant: humble; shy*

14. **nemesis** (nem´ i sis) *n.* someone or something a person cannot
    conquer or achieve; a hated enemy
    Sherlock Holmes tried to outwit his *nemesis*, Moriarty.
    syn: rival; adversary   *ant: collaborator; friend*

15. **lethal** (lē´ thəl) *adj.* deadly; fatal
    The clean-up crew wore respirators to protect themselves from the *lethal* vapors.
    syn: mortal   *ant: harmless*

EXERCISE I—Words in Context

From the list below, supply the words needed to complete the paragraph. Some words will not be used.

anachronism	lethal	effusive	gape
holocaust	defunct	embroil	

1. The argument over the reality of global warming _____ many scientists, most of whom disagree. Some claim that global warming will cause a planetary _____ in which nothing will survive. Other scientists claim such _____ theories are meant only to cause worldwide panic. Indeed, they agree that global warming exists, but that it might take thousands of years to cause the climate to become _____. In a thousand years, or even a hundred years, they assert, the processes that cause global warming will be made _____ by new technologies.

From the list below, supply the words needed to complete the paragraph. Some words will not be used.

lackey	denigrate	lament	humane
anachronism	nemesis	defunct	

2. The elderly Carl knew that he was a[n] _____ among the young programmers working in his office. Each time he struggled to send a simple e-mail message, he _____ the death of the typewriter-and-telephone era in which he had spent most of his career. Bitter that the end of his own usefulness approached, Carl often _____ the young programmers for having no concept of how to use their own brains—not calculators—to solve equations or analyze data. Technology had become the programmers' _____, he felt, and had turned him into a dinosaur. Sometimes the young manager and his _____ mused at Carl's outdated experience with punch cards and mainframes, and it fueled Carl's resentment. He couldn't wait to retire.

From the list below, supply the words needed to complete the paragraph. Some words will not be used.

gape	envisage	humane	holocaust
impertinent	haughty	lackey	

3. "You know that it's _____ to stare and make faces," said the nanny in a[n] _____ tone. "_____ yourself in the same situation. How would you feel if every child who passed _____ at you as though you were a sideshow attraction? Learn to be a little more _____ toward your fellow man."

EXERCISE II—Sentence Completion

Complete the sentence in a way that shows you understand the meaning of the italicized vocabulary word.

1. George *denigrated* Suzanne by spreading rumors that she...

2. Pat *gaped* when she saw...

3. The character's cell phone was an *anachronism* in the movie because...

4. The famous actor traveled with a group of *lackeys* who...

5. The *haughty* salesman in the upscale jewelry shop told us that...

6. Since my car's manufacturer is now *defunct*, I cannot get...

7. During dinner, it's *impertinent* for you to...

8. The representative at the travel agency said, "*Envisage* yourself...

9. Greg became Aaron's *nemesis* when he...

10. The entire community *lamented* the...

11. When the *effusive* man found a bogus charge on his telephone bill, he...

12. The huge hurricane was a natural *holocaust* that...

13. It is not *humane* to leave your...

14. The devious businessman spread rumors that *embroiled* his...

15. The doctor reassured the patient that the substance she encountered was not *lethal* and that she would...

EXERCISE III—Roots, Prefixes, and Suffixes

Study the entries and answer the questions that follow.

The roots *pot* and *poss* mean "to be able."
The prefix *psych* means "mind."
The root *arm* means "tools" or "arms" (weapons).

1. *Using literal translations as guidance, define the following words without using a dictionary.*

   A. potential   D. psychology
   B. potent   E. alarm
   C. psyche   F. disarm

2. If no one can make the journey, it is said to be _____. An *impotent* worker is _____ to do a good job.

3. List as many words as you can think of that contain the roots *poss, pot,* and *arm*.

EXERCISE IV—Inference

Complete the sentences by inferring information about the italicized word from its context.

1. The teacher prefers to *denigrate* her students rather than...

2. If high tariffs on all goods *embroil* the colonists with the mother country, the colonists might...

3. Since the cave contained *lethal* amounts of poison gas, the rescuers had to...

EXERCISE V—Writng

Here is a writing prompt similar to the one you will find on the writing portion of the SAT.

Plan and write an essay based on the following statement:

The world is a dangerous place, not because of those who do evil, but because of those who look on and do nothing.

–Albert Einstein

Assignment: In an essay, indicate whether you agree or disagree with Albert Einstein's assertion about the origins of danger in the world. Is the world dangerous because of evil-doers or because of people who take no action? Support your opinion using evidence from history, current events, literature, or your experience.

Thesis: Write a one-sentence response to the assignment. Make certain this single sentence offers a clear statement of your position.

Example: Albert Einstein's idea that indifferent people are responsible for the dangers in the world is correct because the world will always have evil people, and the only way to stop them is for everyone else to take action.

Organizational Plan: If your thesis is the point on which you want to end, where does your essay need to begin? List the points of development that are inevitable in leading your reader from your beginning point to your end point. This list is your outline.

Draft: Use your thesis as both your beginning and your end. Following your outline, write a good first draft of your essay. Remember to support all your points with examples, facts, references to reading, etc.

Review and Revise: Exchange essays with a classmate. Using the scoring guide for Development on page 222, score your partner's essay (while he or she scores yours). Focus on the development of ideas and use of language conventions. If necessary, rewrite your essay to improve the development and/or your use of language.

Identifying Sentence Errors

Identify the grammatical error in each of the following sentences. If the sentence contains no error, select answer choice E.

1. If Jaanine's sweater <u>was made</u> of better material, <u>it</u> <u>wouldn't have,</u>
                   (A)   (B)   (C)
    frayed <u>so easily</u>.   <u>No error</u>
          (D)   (E)

2. <u>Jenna always argues</u> with <u>her dad</u> because they never <u>agree to</u>
         (A)   (B)   (C)
    <u>each other</u> about anything.   <u>No error</u>
        (D)   (E)

3. Fishermen <u>must handle</u> bait <u>very carefully</u> <u>because</u>
                (A)   (B)   (C)
    <u>you could get stuck</u> on the hook.   <u>No error</u>
        (D)   (E)

4. The <u>most perfect ending</u> of the <u>well-publicized movie</u> we
          (A)   (B)
    <u>attended was</u> a great surprise <u>to us</u>.   <u>No error</u>
      (C)   (D)   (E)

5. My <u>advise</u> to you is <u>to go down</u> to the police station and
        (A)   (B)
    surrender <u>before this</u> gets <u>any more</u> complicated.   <u>No error</u>
          (C)   (D)   (E)

Improving Sentences

The underlined portion of each sentence below contains some flaw. Select the answer choice that best corrects the flaw.

6. Mental illness is diverse and complicated not only <u>to analyze but for assessing.</u>
    A. to assess and for analysis.
    B. to analyze but also to assess.
    C. for assessing but also to analyze.
    D. for analysis but also to assess.
    E. for assessment and analysis.

7. The basic disagreement behind all court cases <u>are usually the same.</u>
    A. is always the same.
    B. are similar.
    C. are basically the same disagreement.
    D. is usually the same.
    E. are never the same.

8. <u>Singers may dislike certain song lyrics, but that doesn't prove they are good or bad.</u>
    A. Singers dislike using lyrics in songs but that doesn't prove they are good or bad.
    B. Even though singers disapprove of song lyrics they sing them, good or bad.
    C. A singer's dislike for certain song lyrics does not prove that the lyrics are good or bad.
    D. Good song lyrics or bad song lyrics, some singers dislike certain ones.
    E. Certain song lyrics are good or bad, but some singers may dislike them.

9. <u>The football team in their new uniforms, as well as the cheerleaders, and the exciting band music.</u>
    A. The football team and the cheerleaders were in their new uniforms, and the band music was exciting.
    B. The cheerleaders, the football team, and the band music was exciting in their new uniforms.
    C. The band music was exciting as well as the football team in their new uniforms as well as the cheerleaders.
    D. In their new uniforms as well as the cheerleaders and the exciting band music.
    E. The football team and cheerleaders in their new uniforms with exciting band music.

10. <u>The landlord denied the many charges that had been made against him, quickly and emphatically</u>.
    A. Quickly and emphatically, the many charges that had been made against the landlord were denied.
    B. The many charges that had been made against the landlord quickly and emphatically, were denied.
    C. Quickly and emphatically denied many charges had been made against the landlord.
    D. Emphatically and quickly the many charges that had been made against the landlord were denied.
    E. The landlord quickly and emphatically denied the many charges that had been made against him.

Lesson Fourteen

1. **catalyst**   (kat´ əl ist)   *n.*   a person, thing, or agent that speeds up or stimulates a result, reaction, or change
    The atom bomb was a *catalyst* in ending World War II.
    syn: mechanism; vehicle; means

2. **jargon**   (jär´ gən)   *n.*   vocabulary distinctive to a particular group of people
    Joe heard the attorneys exchanging legal *jargon*, but he understood little of it.
    syn: terminology; lingo

3. **judicious**   (joō dish´ əs)   *adj.*   showing sound judgment
    A *judicious* manager avoids favoritism and treats everyone the same way.
    syn: sensible; wise; careful   *ant: foolish; impractical; prejudicial*

4. **foible**   (foi´ bəl)   *n.*   a minor weakness in character
    The chef's only *foible* was her forgetfulness.
     syn: fault; shortcoming

5. **benediction**   (ben i dik´ shən)   *n.*   the act of blessing
    We bowed our heads for the *benediction* before singing the closing hymn.
    ant: curse; malediction

6. **frivolous**   (friv´ ə ləs)   *adj.*   trivial; silly
    They wasted time arguing over a *frivolous* matter.
    syn: inconsequential; vain   *ant: vital; important*

7. **alacrity**   (ə lak´ ri tē)   *n.*   liveliness; willingness; eagerness
    He performed his chores with *alacrity* and finished them before noon.
    syn: enthusiasm; readiness; zeal   *ant: slowness; reluctance*

8. **deify**   (dē´ ə fī)   *v.*   to make a god of; to look upon or worship as a god
    He *deified* her, but he soon discovered that she was as human as anyone else.
    syn: idolize; worship   *ant: abhor; detest*

9. **carnage**   (kär´ nij)   *n.*   bloody and extensive slaughter
    United Nations forces were deployed to end the *carnage* in the war-torn nation.
    syn: bloodshed; slaughter

10. **impel** (im pel´) *v.* push into motion
The man's thirst *impelled* him to continue walking along the desert highway.
syn: urge; force; propel; drive   *ant: restrain*

11. **epitaph** (ep´ i taf) *n.* an inscription on a tombstone; a brief comment about a deceased person
The tombstone had the simple *epitaph*, "Rest In Peace."

12. **harp** (härp) *v.* to persist in talking continuously (on or about something)
My parents *harp* on the importance of completing homework.
syn: ramble; complain

13. **lateral** (lat´ ər əl) *adj.* of or relating to the side
Bill made a *lateral* career move by taking a new job with no change in salary.
syn: sideways

14. **pallid** (pal´ id) *adj.* pale; faint in color
The patient's *pallid* face and labored breathing concerned the doctor.
syn: colorless   *ant: hearty; robust*

15. **impetuous** (im pech´ ōō əs) *adj.* acting suddenly without thought
Impetuous behavior can be hazardous to your health.
syn: impulsive; rash   *ant: planned; careful*

EXERCISE I—Words in Context

From the list below, supply the words needed to complete the paragraph. Some words will not be used.

frivolous	impetuous	deify	catalyst
foible	harp	alacrity	

1. Steve never realized it, but his single _____ was his _____ in complaining about _____ things that do not even bother most people; for example, if a waiter brought Steve the wrong beverage, Steve _____ about the mistake for days. Luckily, he was not so _____ as to cause embarrassing scenes in public.

From the list below, supply the words needed to complete the paragraph. Some words will not be used.

deify	**jargon**	**epitaph**	**harp**
carnage	**pallid**	**impel**	

2. Bonnie was an apprentice, so she didn't understand all the archaeological _____ spoken around the dig site; however, she did understand the theories as to what the farmer had discovered. Statues found near an altar suggested that the ancient tribe used to _____ certain animals and worship them in ceremonies. A large amount of fractured skeletal remains at the dig site suggested that the tribe was also particularly violent; Bonnie's face grew _____ when she paused to think about the _____ that had taken place at the ancient site. The remains of hundreds of people lay in the sacrificial pit without a single marker or _____ to mark their resting place.

From the list below, supply the words needed to complete the paragraph. Some words will not be used.

benediction	**judicious**	**foible**	**catalyst**
lateral	**impel**	**alacrity**	

3. Lynn never personally enjoyed working in the family business, but she was the _____ responsible for transforming the company's _____ moves into huge profit margins. For years, she had spoken of leaving the business, hoping that the threat would _____ her father to seek a good replacement for her, but he never did. At dinner one evening, shortly after the _____, Lynn announced that she had been offered a job with a larger company at twice her current salary. To Lynn's surprise, her father congratulated her and complimented her for making a[n] _____ decision.

EXERCISE II—Sentence Completion

Complete the sentence in a way that shows you understand the meaning of the italicized vocabulary word.

1. Since you made an *impetuous* remark to the restaurant manager, I don't want to…

2. Too much *lateral* stress on the telephone pole caused it to…

3. They could not read the *epitaph* because…

4. Few could imagine the *carnage* that had taken place at…

5. For summer help at the factory, the boss wanted teenagers with the *alacrity* to…

6. After the reverend gave the *benediction*, everyone at the banquet…

7. The broker made a series of *judicious* investments that…

8. The new quarterback was the *catalyst* for the team's…

9. Pat's face turned *pallid* when…

10. Ken put on headphones because he could no longer stand to hear Mike *harp* about…

11. The onset of war *impelled* many people to…

12. The ancient civilization *deified* their priests; regular citizens were not even allowed to…

13. The used car was as ugly in color as it was in shape, but these were only *frivolous* concerns to Clint because he…

14. Though the billionaire gives millions to charity each year, many people refuse to look beyond his odd *foible* of…

15. You should become familiar with nautical *jargon* if you plan to…

EXERCISE III—Roots, Prefixes, and Suffixes

Study the entries and answer the questions that follow.

The roots *stru* and *struct* mean "to build."
The roots *tempor* and *temper* mean "time."
The root *therm* means "heat."

1. Using literal translations as guidance, define the following words without using a dictionary.

   A. thermostat   D. destruct
   B. instrument   E. structure
   C. hypothermia   F. contemporary

2. A *thermometer* measures _____. If you want your coffee to retain its heat, then you might put it in a[n] _____. A branch of science that deals with the study of heat is called _____-dynamics.

3. A[n] _____ worker is hired for a limited time only. In science fiction, a disruption in time might be described as a[n] _____ disturbance.

4. List as many words as you can think of that contain the roots *tempor, temper, stru,* and *struct.*

EXERCISE IV—Inference

Complete the sentences by inferring information about the italicized word from its context.

1. Penny didn't demonstrate the *alacrity* to play soccer, so the coach...

2. Hearing an exciting account about discovering lost treasure might *impel* an inspired listener to...

3. If the boss tells the workmen to ignore any *frivolous* concerns and simply get the job done, then the boss doesn't want the workers to worry about...

EXERCISE V—Critical Reading

Below is a reading passage followed by several multiple-choice questions similar to the ones you will encounter on the SAT. Carefully read the passage and choose the best answer for each of the questions.

The U.S. Fish and Wildlife Service operates the Fisheries Program and has been in existence for over 100 years. Some of the issues that inspired the program's creation are still being addressed today.

1   Americans love fish. We catch them for food, for recreation, and for income. We photograph them, we display them on walls, and we watch them in aquariums. We pursue fish in pristine wilderness and in crowded urban waters; however, habitat degradation, pollution, dams, competition from invasive species, and over-harvesting threaten America's vital aquatic resource.

2   At one time, America's pristine waters supported plentiful and robust fisheries. Our nation's natural treasures appeared to be unlimited until the Industrial Revolution and population surge required vast quantities of natural resources, notably water, timber, minerals, and wildlife. During this period, water quality and fish resources endured a rapid decline.

3   By the mid-1800s, fishermen identified the decrease in fish populations. In 1871, Spencer Fullerton Baird, Assistant Secretary of the Smithsonian Institution, wrote to Congress urging Federal protection for the nation's fisheries. Baird warned that America would lose fish as a way of life and lifestyle, and that such a calamity would leave a series of evils in its wake.

4   In response to threatened fish populations, Congress created the Commission on Fish and Fisheries, which is now called the U.S. Fish and Wildlife Service (FWS). It was the first federal agency dedicated to the conservation of natural resources. The first objective of the commission was to determine whether fisheries had indeed declined and to plot an appropriate course of action.

5   The present Fish and Wildlife Service still upholds the mission to restore our fisheries by surveying populations and habitats, raising native fish and other species, and restoring habitats to meet the goals of fisheries management plans. To fulfill these far-reaching objectives, the Fish and Wildlife Service maintains a network of field stations across the country, including seventy hatcheries and one genetics laboratory.

6   One of the most important objectives of the Fish and Wildlife Service is to moderate declining native fish populations by restoring and protecting habitats and reintroducing fish where appropriate. The FWS also works to recover species listed under the Endangered Species Act by monitoring and evaluating fish populations. Using databases, the FWS conducts long term monitoring to track the health and relative abundance of fish resources; the recorded data can then be used to create the appropriate protective measures to sustain specific ecosystems.

7   In the area of habitat conservation and management, the Fish and Wildlife Service determines habitat needs for fish populations and identifies necessary

improvements. Because dams and other man-made barriers threaten many fish populations, the program works with other federal, state, and local agencies to advocate high water quality and availability of passage in streams and rivers.

8   The Fish and Wildlife Service also provides leadership in the development and application of state-of-the-art science and technology for conservation of fish and other aquatic species. Fish health centers inspect hatchery fish for pathogens, diagnose diseases, and then recommend remedial treatments to improve fish health management. Some wild fish, such as the endangered Pacific salmon, require close health monitoring to ensure their recovery. This monitoring also prevents species from becoming threatened or endangered.

9   The Fish and Wildlife Service is a government organization, but that does not mean that it interacts exclusively with other government agencies. It is currently working in partnership with Native American Tribal Nations to restore fish and wildlife, thereby improving capacity for fishing and hunting. Cooperation between the Fish and Wildlife Service and the White Mountain Apache Tribe, for example, has already been successful in recovering the once-endangered Apache trout. The trout is now on the threatened list instead of the endangered list, and the improvement indicates that the trout and its habitat are almost fully restored.

10   Our American heritage includes a rich history of recreational fishing, and the Fish and Wildlife Service helps ensure its future. In the Southeast alone, the FWS releases more than six million fish in an attempt to enhance sport-fishing opportunities and to mitigate the negative impact of federal dams.

11   Despite a century of progress, America's fish are still in danger. The Fish and Wildlife Service is more important than ever as aquatic habitats decline due to erosion, sedimentation, altered stream flows, dams, obstructions, pollution, and invasive species. Through diligent application of sound science, effective management practices, and dedicated partnerships, the Fish and Wildlife Service will continue to conserve species and their habitats and thus ensure the future of America's fishing tradition.

1. Which of the following best describes the main idea of the passage?
    A. Fishing is an American national pastime, thanks to wildlife management.
    B. Industrialization has reduced the fish population in the United States.
    C. The Fish and Wildlife Service is dedicated to conserving fish and their habitats.
    D. The nation's water quality has declined.
    E. The Fish and Wildlife Service creates recreational fishing opportunities.

2. As used in paragraph 3, *fisheries* most nearly means
    A. places in which fish are raised by people.
    B. places in which fish are stored.
    C. lakes and ponds.
    D   places in which fish are caught.
    E. coastal fishing regions.

3. Which of the following events led to a decline in fish population?
    A. the Industrial Revolution
    B. the Civil War
    C. illegal fishing practices
    D. acidic water conditions due to mine drainage
    E. the inaction of Spencer Fullerton Baird

4. According to the passage, which of the following is *not* a technique used by the Fish and Wildlife Service to restore fisheries?
    A. surveying populations
    B. restoring habitats
    C. predicting pollution trends
    D. raising native fish
    E. surveying habitats

5. The author notes that the Fish and Wildlife Service helps the White Mountain Apache Tribe, which shows
    A. the tribe's food supply was vanishing.
    B. the Apache trout is the most popular sport fish in the United States.
    C. the agency also works with groups outside the government.
    D. concern for the Native American Tribal Nations.
    E. the tribe will convince Congress to allocate more funds to the Fish and Wildlife Service.

6. According to the passage, which answer places the terms in the order of best to worst?
    A. extinct, threatened, endangered
    B. endangered, extinct, threatened
    C. threatened, extinct, endangered
    D. threatened, endangered, extinct
    E. endangered, threatened, extinct

7. Which of the following is *not* a present danger to fish habitats?
    A. sport fishing
    B. sediment in water supplies
    C. the rerouting of waterways
    D. industrial waste
    E. dam building

8. Which of the following best describes the tone of the passage?
    A. lively and entertaining
    B. thoughtful and optimistic
    C. droll and witty
    D. scholarly and substantial
    E. dry and unemotional

9. Which of the following would be an appropriate title for this passage?
    A. Native and Aquatic Nuisance Species
    B. Leadership in Aquatic Natural Science
    C. Preserving America's Fisheries
    D. Aquatic Habitat Conservation and Management
    E. U.S. Fishery Resources

10. This passage would most likely be found in a/an
    A. encyclopedia.
    B. popular fishing newsletter.
    C. academic journal.
    D. science textbook.
    E. newspaper.

REVIEW

Lessons 8 – 14

EXERCISE I – Sentence Completion

Choose the best pair of words to complete the sentence. Most choices will fit grammatically and will even make sense logically, but you must choose the pair that best fits the idea of the sentence.

Note that these words are not taken directly from lessons in this book. This exercise is intended to replicate the sentence completion portion of the SAT.

1. Each year, thousands of cold-weather _____ flock to Germany to test their _____ in what is the longest cross-country skiing race in the world.
    A. enthusiasts, endurance
    B. participants, abilities
    C. fans, skill
    D. professionals, greatness
    E. aficionados, bravado

2. The old adage, "One picture is worth a thousand words," is frequently disputed by authors who _____ that one word _____ up a thousand pictures.
    A. contend, conjures
    B. sermonize, calls
    C. assert, sets
    D. postulate, summons
    E. presuppose, evokes

3. _____ of the _____ attitudes towards violence and vulgarity on television is the introduction of new technologies to censor what a viewer might see, and address the ever-changing tastes of American families.
    A. Symptomatic, evolving
    B. Emblematic, disparate
    C. Symbolic, modern
    D. Salient, shifting
    E. Illustrative, liberal

4. After two nights of _____ and rioting, police finally brought a semblance of order to the _____ community.
   A. damage, calmed
   B. rage, disputed
   C. darkness, horrible
   D. restlessness, prosperous
   E. altercations, ravaged

5. Tyrone was _____ of snakes until he actually held one; after that, his fear gave way to a rational understanding of their _____ place in nature.
   A. frightened, sacred
   B. petrified, rightful
   C. fond, scientific
   D. scared, reasonable
   E. terrified, maligned

6. Six-year-old Tommy's _____ became so _____ that he was unable to distinguish the lies from the truth.
   A. stories, realistic
   B. dishonesty, clear
   C. fibbing, ubiquitous
   D. prevarications, complicated
   E. disillusionment, pervasive

7. Of all the _____ on the stage that night, the one Sheri wanted to meet the most was the _____ of the Annual Award for Charitable Donations.
   A. stars, winner
   B. trendsetters, author
   C. philanthropists, recipient
   D. notables, humanitarian
   E. dignitaries, designer

8. _____ from the hurricane included downed power lines and broken gas mains, which _____ the entire community.
   A. Indications, beleaguered
   B. Complications, endangered
   C. Destruction, damaged
   D. Damage, hurt
   E. Situations, threatened

EXERCISE II – Crossword Puzzle

Use the clues to complete the crossword puzzle. The answers consist of vocabulary words from lessons 8 through 14.

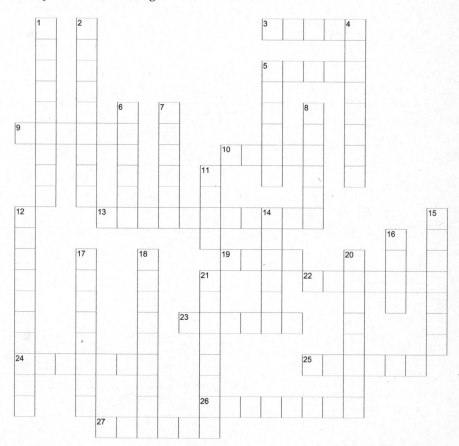

Across
3. push into motion
5. to pretend
9. useless; pointless
10. feeling of uneasiness
13. one who receives benefits
19. something that covers or conceals
22. no longer in existence
23. slavish follower
24. to draw into a fight
25. minor weakness in character
26. beginner
27. to stop

Down
1. acting suddenly without thought
2. associate; partner
4. to become weak; to lose strength
5. loud quarrel
6. to scold or rebuke
7. to hinder, obstruct
8. sermon
11. manner of walking
12. shameless boldness
14. to hint at
15. warlike; military
16. cause of ruin
17. easily angered
18. trivial; silly
20. emotionally excessive
21. glaringly bad; outrageous

Lesson Fifteen

1. **adjunct** (aj´ ungkt) *adj.* connected or attached to in a dependent, subordinate, or auxiliary manner, but not a part of
    Dr. Jones, who teaches only one class, is an *adjunct* faculty member at the university, not a full professor.

2. **macabre** (mə käb´) *adj.* horrible; grim
    The *macabre* paintings featured torture scenes from the Spanish Inquisition.
    syn: ghastly; sinister   *ant: beautiful; lovely*

3. **farcical** (fär´ si kəl) *adj.* absurd; ridiculously clumsy
    The botched bank robbery became *farcical* when the getaway car broke down.
    syn: ludicrous; funny   *ant: somber; serious*

4. **debonair** (deb ə nâr´) *adj.* carefree and self-confident in manner; elegant and gracious
    I expected to see an awkward young man, but instead I saw a *debonair* gentleman.
    syn: charming; refined; suave   *ant: gauche; awkward*

5. **penchant** (pen´ chənt) *n.* a strong liking
    She had a *penchant* for tiny, nervous dogs with high-pitched barks.
    syn: fondness; inclination; taste   *ant: dislike; abhorrence*

6. **deplete** (di plēt´) *v.* to use up gradually
    If we *deplete* our limited food supply, we will have to hunt for food.
    syn: empty; exhaust   *ant: replenish*

7. **chicanery** (shi kā´ nə rē) *n.* the use of tricks or clever talk to deceive or evade
    The con artist used old-fashioned *chicanery* to steal credit card information.
    syn: trickery; subterfuge   *ant: honesty*

8. **feisty** (fī´ stē) *adj.* aggressive; lively; energetic
    The tiger cub was small but *feisty*, so we approached him with caution.
    syn: spirited; frisky   *ant: lethargic*

9. **mitigate** (mit´ i gāt) *v.* to make less severe; to become milder
    Gary put plywood over the windows to *mitigate* any damage that the hurricane might do to his house.
    syn: diminish; alleviate   *ant: aggravate; exacerbate*

10. **gull** (gul) *v.* to cheat; to fool or hoax
The man in the carnival booth *gulled* me out of twenty dollars.
syn: dupe; scam; trick

11. **nadir** (nā´ dər) *n.* lowest point
Getting fired was the *nadir* of Bob's terrible week.
syn: bottom   *ant: peak; zenith*

12. **equivocal** (i kwiv´ ə kəl) *adj.* ambiguous; intentionally vague
His answer was *equivocal*, despite my plea for a simple "Yes" or "No."
syn: uncertain; cryptic   *ant: certain; definite*

13. **genealogy** (jē nē al´ ə jē) *n.* family history
The family tree depicted his *genealogy*.
syn: lineage

14. **impervious** (im pûr´ vē əs) *adj.* incapable of being affected
The wounded soldier, apparently *impervious* to pain, continued to fight.
syn: resistant; invulnerable   *ant: vulnerable*

15. **filial** (fil´ ē əl) *adj.* of, relating to, or befitting a son or daughter
They were not related, but Sam had a *filial* respect for his mentor.

EXERCISE I—Words in Context

From the list below, supply the words needed to complete the paragraph. Some words will not be used.

deplete	feisty	equivocal	gull
mitigate	chicanery	filial	

1. In an effort to _____ costs, the Lockwoods hired their neighbor, Bob, to install a new roof on their house. When Bob, a carpenter, had heard that the Lockwoods needed a new roof on their house, he advised them not to let some contractor _____ them into paying for something they didn't need. The existing roof needed only a simple repair, Bob said, and there was no need for the Lockwoods to _____ their savings for unnecessary construction. Bob knew that some so-called discount contractors frequently used _____ and _____ estimates to cheat clients.

From the list below, supply the words needed to complete the paragraph. Some words will not be used.

feisty	debonair	chicanery	genealogy
nadir	penchant	farcical	

2. Oscar Wilde's _____ for satire shows in his play, The Importance of Being Earnest. This energetic play is a[n] _____ comedy in which _____ characters depict the expectedly refined, _____ members of the Victorian upper class as clumsy, erratic fools. At the end of the play, the two central characters, who are friends, discover that they share the same _____ and that they are actually brothers.

From the list below, supply the words needed to complete the paragraph. Some words will not be used.

mitigate	macabre	adjunct	farcical
impervious	filial	nadir	

3. Frank thought that a camping trip might be a good way to improve his _____ standing with his son and daughter, whom he rarely saw due to his long work hours. He planned a hike through the _____ of a canyon and then picked out a nice spot on the map where they could pitch tents for the night and tell _____ stories around the campfire. Frank thought that the kids would jump at the idea; unfortunately, they did not.

   "Dad," moaned Tim, "you know that I'm busy this weekend." Frank looked as if he were listening to his son, but he was actually _____ to the protest.

   "Oh, come on," said Frank, automatically. "We'll have a great time. I used to be a[n] _____ counselor for a camp—"

   "A *basketball* camp," interrupted Lisa. "And everyone knows that basketball camps are exactly where people go to learn wilderness survival skills."

EXERCISE II—Sentence Completion

Complete the sentence in a way that shows you understand the meaning of the italicized vocabulary word.

1.   One *macabre* room at the haunted house contained…

2.   The *debonair* hero of the novel waltzed right into the villain's hideout and…

3.   If we *deplete* the Earth's natural resources too soon, the world will…

4.   Bill broke his arm when the *feisty* horse…

5.   Police put out a warning for a man who *gulls* people by claiming to be…

6.   Tony's *equivocal* answer to our question only caused…

7.   After years of being the new kid at school, Dawn became *impervious* to…

8.   Janice is a full-time writer, but in the evenings, she is an *adjunct* instructor at…

9.   Barbara was tired of watching *farcical* movies, so she decided…

10.   Mary-Ellen had a *penchant* for the outdoors, so for her vacation, she…

11.   The used-car salesman sometimes used *chicanery* to…

12.   One way to *mitigate* the swelling of a sprained ankle is to…

13.   During the *nadir* of her career, Tina…

14.   The chart in the history book shows the *genealogy* of…

15.   On the frontier, if parents had to leave their homestead, it was a *filial* duty for the children to…

EXERCISE III—Roots, Prefixes, and Suffixes

Study the entries and answer the questions that follow.

The suffix *ion* means "the act of."
The root *cret* means "to separate," "to decide," or "to distinguish."
The root *spir* means "to breathe."

1.   Using literal translations as guidance, define the following words without using a dictionary.

   A. secretary   D. spirit
   B. excrete   E. conspire
   C. secretion   F. inspiration

2.   The government might mark certain information as being _____ to distinguish it from ordinary information. People who have the special information must use _____ in deciding who receives it, because a leak could compromise national security.

3.   Someone who needs help breathing might use a[n] _____. A story that breathes life into you might be said to _____ you.

4.   List as many words as you can think of that contain the suffix *ion*.

EXERCISE IV—Inference

Complete the sentences by inferring information about the italicized word from its context.

1.   If you have a *penchant* for working with children because they like to learn, then you might...

2.   Two extra lodgers during the winter in the mountains might cause you to *deplete* your food supply quickly, so before winter, you should...

3.   If the prisoner appears to be *impervious* to rehabilitation, the parole board will probably...

EXERCISE V—Writing

Here is a writing prompt similar to the one you will find on the writing portion of the SAT.

Plan and write an essay based on the following statement:

That all men are equal is a proposition to which, at ordinary times, no sane individual has ever given his assent.

–Aldous Huxley, *Proper Studies*

Assignment: Conflicting perspectives of human equality have been a source of unrest for thousands of years, but Aldous Huxley claims that no normal person would ever admit that all people are equal. Does Huxley's quote apply to mankind as a whole or individually? In an essay, indicate whether you agree or disagree with Huxley, explain his quote, and then explain the level of human existence to which it is supposed to apply.

Thesis: Write a one-sentence response to the assignment. Make certain this single sentence offers a clear statement of your position.

Example: Aldous Huxley's suggestion that not all people are equal is correct, because there are certain things that some people can do that others can't, no matter how hard they might try.

Organizational Plan: If your thesis is the point on which you want to end, where does your essay need to begin? List the points of development that are inevitable in leading your reader from your beginning point to your end point. This list is your outline.

Draft: Use your thesis as both your beginning and your end. Following your outline, write a good first draft of your essay. Remember to support all your points with examples, facts, references to reading, etc.

Review and Revise: Exchange essays with a classmate. Using the scoring guide for Sentence Formation and Variety on page 223, score your partner's essay (while he or she scores yours). Focus on the sentence structure and use of language conventions. If necessary, rewrite your essay to improve the sentence structure and/or your use of language.

Improving Paragraphs

Read the following passage and then answer the multiple-choice questions that follow. The questions will require you to make decisions regarding the revision of the reading selection.

(1) The thunderhead, with its spires reaching miles into the evening sky, cast a shadowy curtain on the shoreline as the sun settled below the opposite horizon. (2) Helios retreated from Poseidon, and for good reason: the approaching fiend was quite possibly the largest tempest to strike the grainy shore in months.

(3) Torrential rain followed the hail. (4) The sand on and near the beach became so saturated with water that streams formed among the weeds and occasionally washed creatures out onto the open beach. (5) Few were able to cling to the sand after one pass of the surging seawater.

(6) The number of scuttling beach residents diminished with the last few rays of light. (7) Most of them were scavengers seeking food scraps from decaying horseshoe crabs, only vaguely aware that something bad approached their community. (8) They made clicking noises as they scurried across the wet sand, over the dunes, and into the tall grass, where it burrowed to hide from the pending onslaught. (9) Storms like this were known to cause flash floods. (10) Those near the water simply disappeared into the rising surf; not one reappeared in the frothing brine that each wave carried further inland. (11) A flock of noisy seagulls concluded their hour-long battle over a wet fast-food bag and allowed the gales to carry them inland, where they huddled beneath the joists of condemned homes and the rafters of corrugated warehouses. (12) They sat silent and inert, as though their instinct to overcome hunger for safety had turned them into an entirely different species. (13) Unlike the rest of the beach life, the birds were safe of the storm.

(14) All but the simplest order of creatures experienced panic when the first wave of hailstones tore through vegetation and threw sand from miniature impact craters. (15) The icy projectiles, some the size of apples, stung the backs of exposed wildlife huddled in the grass. (16) Smaller crustaceans did not fare as well; hail smashed exoskeletons and leg joints. (17) They would become food for their neighbors after the storm.

(18) The worst of the storm lasted only minutes, but it eliminated all but a fraction of the beach colony. (19) Most had been swept into the dark abyss beneath the starless void, and, in their relatively short lives, they would never be able to battle the riptide to return to the sands on which they spent their lives before the storm. (20) Those left in the open, disoriented from tumbling in the surf, would become food for the cackling gang of seagulls when it retuned to continue its feeding frenzy.

1. What change would improve the chronological order of the paragraphs?
    A. Exchange paragraphs 1 and 2.
    B. Exchange paragraphs 2 and 3.
    C. Place paragraph 2 to follow paragraph 4.
    D. Place paragraph 1 to follow paragraph 4.
    E. Delete paragraph 2.

2. Which of the following corrects the grammatical error in sentence 8?
    A. Replace *where it burrowed* with *where they burrowed*.
    B. Replace *they* with *horseshoe crabs*.
    C. Replace the comma after *grass* with a semicolon.
    D. Capitalize *dunes*.
    E. Delete *across*.

3. If the passage had to be shortened, which sentence could be removed without harming the intent of the passage?
    A. sentence 6
    B. sentence 7
    C. sentence 8
    D. sentence 9
    E. sentence 10

4. Which of the following best improves the underlined portion of sentence 13?

    Unlike the rest of the beach life, <u>the birds were safe of the storm</u>.

    A. the birds were saved from the storm.
    B. the birds were safe.
    C. the birds would be saved from the storm.
    D. the birds had safe during the storm.
    E. the birds were safer.

5. Which change would best make paragraph 3 easier to read?
    A. Delete sentence 6.
    B. Exchange paragraph 3 with paragraph 5.
    C. Include more descriptions of seagulls.
    D. Begin a new paragraph after sentence 10.
    E. Begin a new paragraph after sentence 11.

Lesson Sixteen

1. **daub** (dôb) *v.* to paint coarsely or unskillfully
Painting requires patience and consistency; you cannot simply *daub* the wood with a paint-laden brush.
syn: smear

2. **admonish** (ad mon´ ish) *v.* to warn; to caution in counsel
The lifeguard *admonished* the children for swimming beyond the buoys.
syn: advise; notify; warn

3. **obeisance** (ō bā´ səns) *n.* a bow or similar gesture expressing deep respect
The villager rendered *obeisance* as the king's entourage passed.

4. **cache** (kash) *n.* a concealed store of goods or valuables
While the campers were canoeing on the lake, bears raided their *cache*.
syn: hoard; reserve

5. **affliction** (ə flik´ shən) *n.* anything causing great suffering
Heatstroke can be a lethal *affliction* if not treated.
syn: difficulty; pain; burden   *ant: relief; aid*

6. **mendicant** (men´ di kənt) *n.* a beggar
The tourists tried to avoid the *mendicants* sitting in front of the gift shop.

7. **aphorism** (af´ ə riz əm) *n.* a concise statement of a truth or principle
My father lives by the *aphorism*, "Waste not, want not."
syn: adage; maxim; saying

8. **oscillate** (os´ ə lāt) *v.* to swing or move back and forth like a pendulum.
Your opinion of the movie will probably *oscillate* from good to bad until you have more time to think about it.
syn: vacillate; fluctuate; alternate

9. **delete** (di lēt´) *v.* to take out; to remove
You can *delete* the third sentence because it is unnecessary.
syn: erase; cancel   *ant: include; add*

10. **oust** (oust) *v.* to drive out; expel; deprive
The bailiff *ousted* the noisy courtroom spectators.
syn: eject

11. **impermeable** (im pûr´ mē ə bəl) *adj.* not permitting passage (especially of fluids)
The parka has an *impermeable* layer that keeps you dry.
syn: impenetrable; impervious   *ant: permeable*

12. **paean** (pē´ an) *n.* a fervent expression, or song, of joy or praise
The book is simply a *paean* to the candidate; it lists his achievements, but not his failures.
syn: acclaim; tribute

13. **imperturbable** (im pər tûr´ bə bəl) *adj.* not easily excited, even under pressure
The captain's *imperturbable* manner during the storm reassured the worried sailors.
syn: collected; unflustered

14. **lax** (laks) *adj.* careless or negligent
Don't become too *lax* in your studies, or you'll fail.
syn: slack; neglectful   *ant: careful; meticulous*

15. **palpable** (pal´ pə bəl) *adj.* obvious; capable of being touched or felt
The fear in the room was so *palpable* that Tim thought he could taste it.
syn: evident; conspicuous   *ant: obscure; unclear*

EXERCISE I—Words in Context

From the list below, supply the words needed to complete the paragraph. Some words will not be used.

admonish	affliction	lax	imperturbable
delete	obeisance	oust	

1. Everyone knew that Kiplar was an outsider when he failed to give _____ to the passing Queen. One of the royal escorts immediately spotted Kiplar and walked over to _____ him for his failure to show respect.
   "What is this _____ of yours that prevents you from taking a knee upon sight of our queen? Shall we _____ you from your sleepy village and see how you fare in a dungeon?" The guard's threat did not faze the _____ man. Kiplar, still standing, simply smiled.

From the list below, supply the words needed to complete the paragraph. Some words will not be used.

paean	aphorism	impermeable	affliction
palpable	lax	daub	

2. Justin began to have second thoughts about his summer job when the temperature rose to ninety degrees. For the third day in a row, he stood on a flimsy ladder and _____ maroon paint onto the side of Mrs. Bailey's house. He wore no gloves today; yesterday, he discovered that the cheap cotton painter's gloves were not _____ when he removed them and found his hands stained maroon. To make matters worse, Mrs. Bailey frequently came outside to ensure that Justin hadn't become _____ on the job. The old _____, "time flies when you're having fun," couldn't have been more applicable to Justin, because each ten-hour day of painting felt like an eternity. If hard work builds character, thought Justin, then he should have a[n] _____ amount of character after this job.

From the list below, supply the words needed to complete the paragraph. Some words will not be used.

paean	delete	oust	mendicant
cache	oscillate	palpable	

3. In the late afternoon, Marvin opened the bottom drawer of his desk to reveal a[n] _____ of snack cakes and little bags of potato chips. He helped himself to a cream-filled cupcake as he perused old e-mail messages and _____ any old ones that were just taking up space on the computer's hard drive. A heavy fan _____ in the corner of the office, causing self-adhesive notes and thumb-tacked comic strips to flap around in the breeze every few seconds. Next to the fan was a tied trash bag full of empty aluminum soda cans for Joe, a[n] _____ who lived in the alley behind the magazine publisher. Joe, who chose the streets over shelters, inspired many people at the office, and he had no idea that Marvin's next article was going to be a[n] _____ to the homeless who have learned to sustain themselves despite their austere living conditions.

EXERCISE II—Sentence Completion

Complete the sentence in a way that shows you understand the meaning of the italicized vocabulary word.

1.   The sprinkler head *oscillates* so that the entire lawn…

2.   The book began with the old *aphorism*, "…

3.   The magazine editor told the writer to *delete*…

4.   A *mendicant* outside the grocery store asked me…

5.   Bouncers at the club *ousted* Herbert because he…

6.   The arctic explorers could not find their *cache* of supplies because…

7.   If you wear boots that are *impermeable*, you won't have to worry about…

8.   The *affliction* became widespread when villagers drank water from…

9.   The National Anthem is a *paean* to…

10. The young student bowed his head in *obeisance* to…

11. The old, *imperturbable* dog lay on the floor and let the puppies…

12. I'll *admonish* you this time, but the next time you do it, I'm going to…

13. The *lax* worker at the power plant failed to notice that…

14. During the funeral, Amy *daubed*…

15. Your promises are great, but if you don't show some *palpable* progress on the project, the teacher will…

EXERCISE III—Roots, Prefixes, and Suffixes

Study the entries and answer the questions that follow.

The roots *liber* and *liver* mean "free."
The root *soph* means "wise."
The root *men* means "to think."

1.   *Using literal translations as guidance, define the following words without using a dictionary.*

     A.   philosophy   D.   liberty
     B.   sophomore   E.   liberate
     C.   mental   F.   demented

2.   A person who has lived a complex life and gathered wisdom might be described as being _____.

3.   List as many words as you can think of that contain the roots *liber, liver,* or *men.*

EXERCISE IV—Inference

Complete the sentences by inferring information about the italicized word from its context.

1.   If someone has an *affliction* that affects his or her legs, then that person might...

2.   Pirates might hide their *cache* of stolen goods so that...

3.   A security camera might be designed to *oscillate* in order to...

EXERCISE V—Critical Reading

Below is a pair of reading passages followed by several multiple-choice questions similar to the ones you will encounter on the SAT. Carefully read both passages and choose the best answer to each of the questions.

The authors of the following passages discuss the Tunguska event of 1908, in which a strange object exploded with devastating force in the sky over Siberia.

Passage 1

1 In the quest to find answers to unexplained mysteries, there are times to be skeptical and times to be creative. The explanation of the Tunguska explosion of 1908 requires creativity, unless skeptics actually find some physical evidence.

2 On the morning of June 30th, 1908, residents near the remote Tunguska River, Siberia, witnessed what was doubtlessly the largest, unexplained cataclysmic event of the twentieth century. According to the many eyewitnesses, a blazing, white light—brighter than lightning—streaked across the sky, pulling a tail hundreds of miles in length. Suddenly, while still airborne, the mysterious object detonated over the forest, setting everything beneath it on fire and sending destructive shock waves and heat throughout a 300-mile radius. The description of the ensuing fireball and mushroom cloud most nearly resembles the modern description of a nuclear explosion; however, nuclear weapons weren't even tested until 1945.

3 People had no doubt that something exploded; seismographs around the world detected shock waves that had traveled through thousands of miles of earth, and the sky over Siberia radiated an unnatural glow well into the evening. Unfortunately, due to the isolated region in which the explosion occurred, and the chaotic political state of Russia at the time, no one conducted a formal investigation of the Tunguska event until 1921. Members of the Russian Meteorological Institute found widespread damage, but they found no meteorite impact craters. The detonation had literally leveled the forest beyond thirteen miles from the center of the blast, and people living in the region reported that witnesses who didn't die from heat or blast effects died instead from symptoms that indicated radiation poisoning.

4 For more than ninety years, many scientists readily attribute the bizarre explosion to an asteroid or comet that exploded before reaching the earth. Others, including some eyewitnesses, are not so ready to assign such natural explanations to the event; there is no impact crater at the epicenter of the explosion, and investigators discovered no fragments, large or small, of what would have been a massive meteorite.

5 The destruction caused by the Tunguska explosion is commensurate with the effects of a forty-megaton nuclear explosion—that's 1000 times more powerful than the Hiroshima bomb. In theory, meteorites could indeed cause the massive degree of destruction, but no one is sure why (or if) a meteoroid would detonate before striking the ground.

6 The exploding comet theory is quickly gaining credibility as an explanation, because a comet made up of ice and dust would not necessarily leave the evidence required to confirm the material of the object; however, the comet theory neglects the vast thermal destruction and the apparent radiation effects of the explosion.

7 Some Tunguska theorists offer an antimatter-annihilation as an explanation. Antimatter in sufficient quantity might yield an explosion resembling that of nuclear origin, complete with the radiation effects; however, few can explain how antimatter would exist—let alone travel—throughout our galaxy without being annihilated well before reaching earth.

8 To many, the antimatter theory might be more credible than the final alternative: a UFO—a spacecraft or missile of extraterrestrial origin—exploded over Tunguska. The craft would have to have been large, of course, to cause such devastation, but without physical evidence of meteors, comets, or an antimatter annihilation, investigators cannot write off such a theory.

9 Nearly a century has passed since the Tunguska explosion. It is time to solve the mystery before the event occurs again, but this time in a populated area. The threat of meteorites and other extraterrestrial bodies striking earth is a growing concern for humanity; we must account for such threats in this new millennium of human existence. The next Tunguska, whether caused by meteorites, antimatter, or even UFOs, might not be so forgiving as to strike in one of the most desolate areas of the planet. If Tunguska was the product of an asteroid, then we need to prove it and create an appropriate means of defense. If Tunguska was something more complicated than an asteroid, which is quite possible, then we've a lot of reading to do and technology to develop.

Passage 2

1 An unparalleled event occurred in the skies over remote Siberia shortly after 7:00 am on June 30th, 1908. Witnesses for miles around, including passengers on a distant train, watched in awe as a blinding white object streaked across the sky for several seconds before exploding in a fireball that would be incomparable for another thirty-seven years, when the atom bomb made its first appearance. The explosion flattened every tree in the forest as far as forty miles from the blast, and simple mountaineers watched as homes, plants, and livestock burst into flames from a rapid surge of intense heat. Inhabitants close to the explosion were thrown through the air like rag dolls, and some of them died as a result of broken bones, severe burns, or a strange sickness that ensued in the following days. Immediately after the blast, rocks rained upon the countryside and dust filled the air, as though a volcano had blown its top. A column of fire, perhaps a mile in width, lit the sky well into the evening. Most witnesses had no idea what had just happened; unfortunately, no one was able to offer them a theory until thirteen years later, when the political climate of Russia finally allowed scientists to make the trek to Tunguska. Expecting to find evidence of a relatively common meteorite strike, the scientists were surprised to find no impact crater or meteorite pieces; however, that is not sufficient evidence to dismiss the theory that an asteroid or similar object was the cause of the event.

2   For years, several theories have circulated about the source of the explosion. Frenzied theorists offer explanations of alien attacks, crashing spaceships, anti-matter reactions, lightning from the earth, and even a disastrous test of an energy weapon built by the eccentric genius, Nikola Tesla. Serious, ongoing research points not to UFOs or low-probability natural phenomena; instead, most scientists attribute the event to an asteroid or a fragment of a comet, both of which are among the few natural objects capable of such devastating explosions.

3   It is not uncommon, according to scientists, for meteoroids and asteroids to explode in earth's atmosphere. Many of the stony objects burn up, but with the extreme temperatures and unknown materials involved, it's not inconceivable that many of the objects simply explode. It is easy to imagine that a particularly large body, perhaps an asteroid weighing more than 100,000 tons, would generate tremendous heat and air pressures while traveling at supersonic speeds through the atmosphere. The heat would be so intense that parts of the asteroid would become superheated plasma, essentially creating an unstable, falling bomb. Extreme air pressures, combined with unstable, superheated compounds, could certainly create the necessary conditions for the object to explode.

4   The comet or asteroid that exploded over Tunguska left little evidence on the scene because it disintegrated upon detonation, spreading materials throughout the atmosphere for hundreds of miles around. How much intact material would remain from a relatively small object in a blast equivalent to that of the largest known thermonuclear weapons? Little, if any.

5   In recent years, researchers have compared the dust at the Tunguska site to the dust found in Antarctica that is known to be from meteorite impacts. The samples are very similar in composition. Scientists also report finding particles imbedded in trees around the site. The particles, they report, are similar to meteorites in composition.

6   It is only a matter of time before the scientific community gathers enough data to prove that the Tunguska explosion was the result of an asteroid or a comet; however, even when that day arrives, irrational skeptics and paranoid green-man watchers will continue to spout theories of exploding warp drives or rare, theoretical, natural phenomena. Perhaps in the future, their day will come and they will have license to say they told us so. Until then, though, we must understand Tunguska as the product of a big rock.

1. The overall tone of the first passage is best described as
    A. concerned.
    B. optimistic.
    C. dolorous.
    D. apologetic.
    E. timid.

2. According to the first passage, where was the object when it exploded?
    A. approximately 300 feet underground
    B. in the upper atmosphere
    C. in the air, over the forest
    D. between two large clouds
    E. on the forest floor

3. According to the first passage, the explosion could not have been an atomic blast because
    A. people had no means of propulsion for nuclear weapons in 1908.
    B. there were no radiation effects among the witnesses.
    C. the treaty banning the use of atomic weapons had been signed.
    D. the Tunguska event predates nuclear testing by nearly forty years.
    E. the Russian Meteorological Institute controlled the only atomic bomb.

4. As used in paragraph 3 of the first passage, *seismograph* refers to
    A. an instrument that alerts people to incoming meteorites.
    B. an instrument that detects variances in light.
    C. an instrument that receives worldwide messages.
    D. an instrument that detects movement of the ground.
    E. an instrument that measures electromagnetic pulse.

5. Why, according to the first passage, must humans develop technology?
    A. to defend the planet from extraterrestrial threats
    B. to better understand the properties of antimatter
    C. so that civilization can colonize other planets if necessary
    D. to make contact with the aliens who attacked Siberia
    E. to prepare for the transition to living in the mines

6. According to paragraph 2 in the second passage, which two groups offer explanations of the Tunguska explosion?
   A. mad scientists and contemporary architects
   B. the Russian Meteorological Institute and the U.S. Department of State
   C. witnesses of the explosion and people on the train
   D. educated workers and local physicians
   E. overzealous thinkers and real scientists

7. According to the second passage, which of the following is *not* a farfetched theory of the Tunguska explosion?
   A. Earth was attacked by an alien weapon.
   B. Tunguska is evidence of time travel.
   C. A piece of a comet exploded.
   D. Tesla conducted a failed test of an energy weapon.
   E. An antimatter annihilation caused the detonation.

8. According to the second passage, which of the following would be categorized as low-probability natural phenomena?
   A. the explosion of an energy weapon
   B. lightning coming from the earth
   C. a fire
   D. a meteorite
   E. an alien torpedo strike

9. What of the following best describes the purpose of the second passage?
   A. disprove alternative theories of the Tunguska explosion
   B. inform readers about new evidence in the Tunguska mystery
   C. respond to the author of the first passage
   D. support the theory that an asteroid or comet caused the Tunguska event
   E. inform readers of the Tunguska event

10. Which of the following best describes similarities between both passages?
    A. Both passages contain a short explanation of antimatter.
    B. Both passages explain the biological effects of radioactivity.
    C. Both passages are intended to frighten readers.
    D. Both passages present the explosion as fact, and both acknowledge several theories of the event.
    E. Both passages contain enough supporting data to prove their points.

11. Which of the following assertions reflects opposition between the two passages?
    A. An asteroid or comet was probably the cause of the Tunguska explosion.
    B. The Tunguska explosion occurred in Siberia.
    C. People died as a result of the Tunguska explosion.
    D. The meteorite that landed in Siberia detonated on the ground.
    E. No one conducted a formal investigation of Tunguska until 1921.

12. Which of the following best describes the use of the term *skeptic* in both passages?
    A. *Skeptic* has a negative connotation in passage 1, and it has a positive connotation in passage 2.
    B. Passage 1 describes skeptics as people who accept simple explanations; passage 2 describes skeptics as people who refuse to accept simple explanations.
    C. Both passages suggest that skeptics are people who refuse to accept unconventional explanations of strange events.
    D. Both passages suggest that skeptics are people who refuse to accept traditional explanations of strange events.
    E. Passage 2 describes skeptics as real scientists, while passage 1 describes skeptics as fanatics.

Lesson Seventeen

1. **pariah** (pə rī´ ə) *n.* a social outcast
   He knew that he would become a *pariah* if anyone saw him in the police car.
   syn: exile; outsider   *ant: insider*

2. **fluent** (flōō´ ənt) *adj.* able to express oneself easily and clearly
   The spy travels with ease because she is *fluent* in four languages.
   syn: well-versed   *ant: inept*

3. **cavort** (kə vôrt´) *v.* to leap about in a sprightly manner; romp
   The children *cavorted* with the puppy in the back yard.
   syn: frolic; prance; caper

4. **pedagogue** (ped´ ə gog) *n.* a schoolteacher
   A single *pedagogue* taught all the children in the rural county.
   syn: educator

5. **melee** (mā´ lā) *n.* a noisy, confused fight
   By the time the police arrived, the *melee* was over.
   syn: skirmish; fracas

6. **ensue** (en sōō´) *v.* to follow as a result
   The monkey escaped from the laboratory, and an epidemic *ensued*.
   syn: to result   *ant: to cause*

7. **desecrate** (des´ i krāt) *v.* to damage a holy place; to treat with irreverence
   The vandals *desecrated* the little church.
   syn: vandalize; violate   *ant: consecrate*

8. **personification** (per son ə fi kā´ shən) *n.* a person or thing that represents an idea
   The old woman was the very *personification* of greed.

9. **bias** (bī´ əs) *n.* a prejudiced view (either for or against); a preference
   The jurors were instructed to review the facts without *bias*.
   syn: partiality; favoritism

10. **aloof** (ə lōōf´) *adj.* reserved, distant
    The teacher remained *aloof* for a few days after arguing with the principal.
    syn: detached; cold; remote   *ant: warm; friendly*

11. **gyrate** (jī´ rāt) *v.* to rotate or revolve quickly; to spiral
     People used to dance, but now they simply *gyrate* in random patterns.
     syn: revolve; whirl

12. **fiat** (fī´ at) *n.* an official order
     The dictator's harsh *fiat* turned the rebels into outlaws.
     syn: decree; authorization

13. **fidelity** (fi del´ i tē) *n.* faithfulness
     The king told his subjects that their *fidelity* would be rewarded.
     syn: loyalty; devotion   *ant: treachery*

14. **rambunctious** (ram bungk´ shəs) *adj.* unruly; uncontrollable
     The *rambunctious* twins kept the house in an uproar from morning until
     night.
     syn: wild; disorderly; boisterous   *ant: calm; pacific; tranquil*

15. **hilarity** (hi lar´ i tē) *n.* gaiety; joviality
     Uncle Harvey's jokes always brought *hilarity* to the family picnics.
     syn: mirth; merriment; glee   *ant: sadness; misery*

EXERCISE I—Words in Context

*From the list below, supply the words needed to complete the paragraph. Some
words will not be used.*

fluent	pariah	desecrate	ensue
fiat	rambunctious	melee	

1. Community outrage _____ when the groundskeeper reported that a
    group of _____ teenagers had _____ the cemetery.
        "What kind of _____ sinks so low as to destroy that which cannot
    be defended?" asked the mayor when told of the crime. "These are memo-
    rials to our forefathers, our families." The mayor, forced to take some type
    of action to prevent such outrageous crimes, issued a[n] _____ man-
    dating a curfew on the small town.

From the list below, supply the words needed to complete the paragraph. Some words will not be used.

bias	aloof	pariah	pedagogue
hilarity	cavort	fluent	

2. The aging _____, a teacher for twenty-two years, was _____ enough in adolescent psychology to know that something was wrong with Anne. The girl normally _____ in the halls and laughed with her friends, but she hadn't spoken a word in week. During class, she remained _____ and stared out the window into a distant field. The teacher's concern was without _____—he genuinely cared about all his students, not just those, like Anne, who made teaching enjoyable.

From the list below, supply the words needed to complete the paragraph. Some words will not be used.

fidelity	hilarity	melee	fiat
personification	gyrate	cavort	

3. Startled by crashing noises coming from the office, Tina ran out of the living room to find her two sons in a[n] _____. Apparently, they were fighting over who was next to spin around in the office chair.
    "You've got hundreds of toys upstairs, and you two fight over who gets to _____ in an office chair?" screamed Tina. "Go play outside—it's a nice day!" As the boys, one six and the other seven, ran into the yard, Tina wondered what would become the next object of conflict. Her boys were the _____ of sibling rivalry—they fought over rights to everything, no matter how silly. The ridiculous disputes were often cause for _____, but too much of it quickly became irritating. Despite the rivalry, Tina didn't question the boys' _____ to one another as brothers; they covered for each other as often as they fought.

EXERCISE II—Sentence Completion

Complete the sentence in a way that shows you understand the meaning of the italicized vocabulary word.

1. The *hilarity* of the celebration was interrupted when...

2. Joe felt like the *pariah* of the class because he...

3. After buying new furniture, Dad warned the *rambunctious* children to...

4. Jan-Tommy is from Norway, but he became *fluent* in English by...

5. The general questioned the *fidelity* of his troops before he ordered them to...

6. Bobby *cavorted* around in the living room until his mom told him that...

7. The king issued a *fiat* which stated that his subjects were to...

8. The *pedagogue* eventually stopped teaching and became the...

9. When the young girl jumped on the table and began to *gyrate* wildly, her mother...

10 Like most action movies, this one featured a big *melee* near the end in which the hero...

11. When Cory began to act very *aloof*, his parents knew that something was wrong because he was usually...

12. Cheering *ensued* when the home team...

13. To eliminate any *bias* from the team selection, judges were chosen from a group of people who had never...

14. Tomb raiders and scavengers *desecrated* the ancient pyramid by...

15. Jerry, who missed the plane that crashed and then bought a winning lottery ticket, is the very *personification* of...

EXERCISE III—Roots, Prefixes, and Suffixes

Study the entries and answer the questions that follow.

The root *tract* means "to draw" or "to dig."
The root *anthro* means "man."
The suffix *ology* means "the study of."
The suffix *oid* means "like."

1. *Using literal translations as guidance, define the following words without using a dictionary.*

    A. intractable   D. zoologist
    B. contract   E. spheroid
    C. biology   F. humanoid

2. The study of man is called _____, and a creature with characteristics that resembles those of man is called a[n] _____.

3. A building *contractor* might need to _____ a foundation before beginning construction. You might find yourself drawn toward a[n] _____ person.

4. List as many words as you can think of that contain the root *tract* and the suffixes *oid* and *ology*.

EXERCISE IV—Inference

Complete the sentences by inferring information about the italicized word from its context.

1. If judges show *bias* in favor of a particular contestant in a beauty pageant, that contestant will probably...

2. The movie villain was described as the *personification* of evil because he...

3. Few people talked to Billy, the *pariah* of the town, because he...

EXERCISE V—Writing

Here is a writing prompt similar to the one you will find on the writing portion of the SAT.

Plan and write an essay based on the following quotation:

> Lives of great men all remind us
>   We can make our lives sublime,
> And, departing, leave behind us
>   Footsteps on the sands of time;
>
> Footsteps, that perhaps another,
>   Sailing o'er life's solemn main,
> A forlorn and shipwrecked brother,
>   Seeing, shall take heart again.
>
> Let us then, be up and doing,
>   With a heart for any fate;
> Still achieving, still pursuing,
>   Learn to labor and to wait.
>
> –Henry Wadsworth Longfellow (1807-1882)
> "A Psalm of Life"

Assignment: Do you agree or disagree with Longfellow's philosophy? In an essay, identify and explain the poem's message about living. Explain why it is legitimate or not, and whether you agree or disagree with it. Support your argument with evidence from your knowledge, reading, experience, or observation.

Thesis: Write a one-sentence response to the assignment. Make certain this single sentence offers a clear statement of your position.

Example: In "A Psalm of Life," Henry Wadsworth Longfellow implies that the only good reason for achieving in life is to provide inspiration for future generations, and this is not a satisfactory reason to achieve.

Organizational Plan: If your thesis is the point on which you want to end, where does your essay need to begin? List the points of development that are inevitable in leading your reader from your beginning point to your end point. This list is your outline.

Draft: Use your thesis as both your beginning and your end. Following your outline, write a good first draft of your essay. Remember to support all your points with examples, facts, references to reading, etc.

Review and Revise: Exchange essays with a classmate. Using the scoring guide for Word Choice on page 224, score your partner's essay (while he or she scores yours). Focus on word choice and the use of language conventions. If necessary, rewrite your essay to improve the word choice and/or your use of language.

Identifying Sentence Errors

Identify the grammatical error in each of the following sentences. If the sentence contains no error, select answer choice E.

1. <u>None of the friends</u> in the <u>lower apartment</u> <u>was injured</u> when the
       (A)   (B)   (C)
    <u>waterbed burst </u>through the ceiling.   <u>No error</u>
         (D)   (E)

2. <u>Bring with you</u> only <u>necessary</u> <u>clothing, leave</u> your blankets
        (A)   (B)   (C)
    <u>at home</u>.   <u>No error</u>
    (D)   (E)

3. <u>Today,</u> <u>less than</u> 25 million Americans <u>work in the fields</u> to
    (A)   (B)   (C)
    produce <u>fruits and vegetables.</u>   <u>No error</u>
          (D)   (E)

4. When I <u>told you</u> I <u>had no plans</u> for the weekend, I did not
          (A)   (B)
    <u>mean to infer</u> that <u>I didn't want to plan</u> anything.   <u>No error</u>
       (C)   (D)   (E)

5. <u>Although</u> she admits <u>she has never seen</u> one, my
       (A)   (B)
    <u>Aunt Margaret says</u> she <u>believes in angles</u> anyway.   <u>No error</u>
       (C)   (D)   (E)

Improving Sentences

The underlined portion of each sentence below contains some flaw. Select the answer choice that best corrects the flaw.

6. Doug took a nasty blow to the head, <u>but may be his condition will improve</u> after he gets a few hours of rest.
    A. but may be his condition will improve
    B. but may be a few hours of rest will improve
    C. but maybe his condition will improve
    D. but his condition will improve
    E. but his maybe condition will improve

7. Anne walked into town hall, made some nasty remarks in front of the mayor, <u>and then she rushes right out to the bus.</u>
    A. then rushes out the door and right onto the bus.
    B. and then rushed right out to the bus.
    C. and the bus was waiting outside, so she jumps on it.
    D. so Anne rushes out and gets on the bus.
    E. then she was rushed right out to the bus.

8. Some women like to wear short skirts, <u>but long dresses are preferred by others.</u>
    A. whereas some do not prefer short skirts.
    B. but sometimes they only wear long dresses.
    C. long dresses are worn by others.
    D. and others are long-dress wearers.
    E. but others prefer long dresses.

9. <u>If our radio is turned on and up all the time and we don't do our homework properly.</u>
    A. If our radio is turned on and up all the time, we don't do our homework properly.
    B. Our homework isn't done properly and if the radio is too loud, it's on all the time.
    C. If our radio is on all the time, and turned up too loud, and we don't do our homework properly.
    D. We don't do our homework properly, and the radio is on all the time and too loud.
    E. We have the radio on all the time and up too loud if we don't do our homework properly.

10. <u>Tiffany and Jeremy fought over the remote control while I tried to read a book noisily.</u>

A. The remote control was fought over noisily by Jeremy and Tiffany while I tried to read a book.

B. Tiffany and Jeremy fought over the remote control while I noisily tried to read a book.

C. Tiffany and Jeremy noisily tried to read a book while I fought over the remote control.

D. Tiffany and Jeremy fought noisily over the remote control while I tried to read a book.

E. I tried to read a book noisily while Tiffany and Jeremy fought over the remote control.

Lesson Eighteen

1. **genocide** (je´ nə sīd) *n.* the deliberate destruction of a group of people
The Nazi *genocide* of millions of Jewish people is a dark time in world history.

2. **zaftig** (zäf´ tig) *adj.* having a full, shapely figure
She knew that she was too *zaftig* to wear the little dress.
syn: curvaceous

3. **predilection** (pre dəl ek´ shən) *n.* a preference toward someone or something
His *predilection* for fast food helped to clog his arteries at an early age.
syn: preference; partiality; penchant   *ant: aversion; hatred*

4. **faux** (fō) *adj.* artificial; false; not genuine
The *faux*-marble countertop is really made of cheap plastic.
syn: fake; imitation   *ant: authentic; true*

5. **foray** (for´ ā) *n.* a surprise attack
The Green Berets conducted a *foray* on the enemy fuel depot.
syn: raid; incursion

6. **conjecture** (kən jek´ chər) *n.* a judgment or opinion based on little or questionable evidence
The defense attorney said that the prosecutor's claims were pure *conjecture*.
syn: speculation; guesswork   *ant: fact*

7. **allocate** (al´ ə kāt) *v.* to distribute, allot, or designate
The government *allocated* the funds for victims of natural disasters.
syn: apportion; assign

8. **gratis** (gra´ təs) *adj.* free; without charge
Tom could have earned ten dollars an hour, but he volunteered to work *gratis*.

9. **materialistic** (mə tir ē əl is´ tik) *adj.* wanting material possessions
The *materialistic* man cared only about keeping up with his neighbors.
          ant: altruistic

10. **belabor** (bi la´ bər) *v.* to work at something beyond practicality; to overstress
    Mom constantly *belabored* the fact that our grades would have to get us through college because her paycheck wouldn't.
    syn: stress; overdo   *ant: disregard; ignore*

11. **progeny** (prä´ jən ē) *n.* offspring; children
    Only a few of the sea turtle's *progeny* will survive predators and live to adulthood.
    syn: descendents; young   *ant: ancestors*

12. **quintessential** (kwin tə sen´ shəl) *adj.* the most typical; ideal
    Johann Sebastian Bach was the *quintessential* Baroque composer.
    syn: model; standard

13. **rudimentary** (rōō də men´ tə rē) *adj.* basic; not refined or well developed
    She claimed to be a great critic despite her *rudimentary* understanding of literature.
    syn: elementary; undeveloped   *ant: refined; sophisticated*

14. **monolithic** (mä nə lith´ ik) *adj.* massive, uniform, and solid
    The *monolithic* monument, made of pure granite, weighed one million tons.

15. **manifesto** (ma nə fes´ tō) *n.* a public declaration of policies or intentions
    The conservation group's *manifesto* declared that its members were opponents of polluting industries.
    syn: proclamation

EXERCISE I—Words in Context

From the list below, supply the words needed to complete the paragraph. Some words will not be used.

rudimentary	predilection	allocate	monolithic
conjecture	quintessential	belabor	

1. Horace attributes his career as a skyscraper window-washer to his
    _____ for being in high places. He also says that the _____ rule
    of the trade is not, "Don't look down," but, "Always attach your safety har-
    ness." Anyone with a[n] _____ knowledge of climbing knows that
    equipment fails and people fall if they haven't taken any precautions.
       "I can't _____ the point enough," said Horace. "Safety, safety,
    safety." After the brief interview, Horace climbed back into his elevator
    scaffold and began the ascent back to the forty-first story of the
    _____ building that he was cleaning this week.

From the list below, supply the words needed to complete the paragraph. Some words will not be used.

gratis	progeny	monolithic	genocide
materialistic	allocate	faux	

2. Cindy was not _____, but she still refused to buy the _____
    leather furniture; she really believed that having plastic furniture was tacky.
    When she _____ a large portion of her savings for purchasing things
    for her new home, she promised herself to buy only items that would retain
    some of their intrinsic, if not monetary, value. The ornate furnishings that
    she ultimately selected would last for a long time, perhaps long enough for
    her _____ to enjoy. After making the substantial purchase, Cindy was
    happy to learn the store would deliver the items to her home _____.

From the list below, supply the words needed to complete the paragraph. Some words will not be used.

zaftig	genocide	quintessential	foray
faux	conjecture	manifesto	

3. Few outsiders knew for sure the condition of the city in the days following the violent revolution, but most _____ described a place of rampant looting and lawlessness after the rebels' _____ on the capital city. Winston, the nearest correspondent, traveled to the city to report the situation, and what he found shocked him. Poor-quality copies of the revolutionaries' _____ hung on bullet-riddled walls next to posters of a smiling, _____ woman advertising a chain of fitness clubs. Orphaned children and distraught mothers roamed the streets as remnants of the near-_____ that had occurred in the weeks leading to the uprising.

EXERCISE II—Sentence Completion

Complete the sentence in a way that shows you understand the meaning of the italicized vocabulary word.

1.   After the accident, the *materialistic* man worried only about…

2.   The ballerina eventually became too *zaftig* to…

3.   You will certainly see *monolithic* structures if you go…

4.   The family *allocated* a portion of its income for…

5.   Every time the kids prepared to go boating, Dad *belabored* them with the importance of…

6.   The world accused the ruler of *genocide* for ordering his army to…

7.   The political party released a *manifesto* that described the party's…

8.   Critics complained that the new book was mostly *conjecture* because it…

9.   Olivia escaped the destitute nation so that her *progeny* might…

10.   Sam had a *predilection* for living in the mountains, so he…

11.   Yvonne's *rudimentary* knowledge of auto repair was not enough for her to…

12.   During the Vikings' *foray*, the surprised villagers…

13.   The *quintessential* teenager spends lots of time…

14.   The *faux* mink coat is actually…

15.   The club thought that the former president would deliver a speech *gratis*, but instead, he…

EXERCISE III—Roots, Prefixes, and Suffixes

Study the entries and answer the questions that follow.

The roots *ped* and *pod* mean "foot."
The root *phob* means "fear."
The root *port* means "to carry" or "bring."

1. Using literal translations as guidance, define the following words without using a dictionary.

    A. import   D. report
    B. transport   E. podiatrist
    C. impede   F. hydrophobia

2. A _____ creature has two legs, a stand with three legs is called a[n] _____, and an animal with four legs is called a[n] _____.

3. If you are afraid of feet, then you might be said to have _____. Someone who fears being in a *claustrum*, or an enclosed space, is said to have _____.

4. List as many words as you can think of that contain the roots *ped, pod,* and *port*.

EXERCISE IV—Inference

Complete the sentences by inferring information about the italicized word from its context.

1. To a *materialistic* person, owning an expensive car might be more important than...

2. The *faux* brick paneling is cheaper than real brick, but it...

3. The scientist's theory was mostly *conjecture*, so the board of directors...

EXERCISE V—Critical Reading

Below is a reading passage followed by several multiple-choice questions similar to the ones you will encounter on the SAT. Carefully read the passage and choose the best answer for each of the questions.

The author of the following passages discusses new trends in the antiques business.

1   Antiques shops are more than just places of business: they are museums in which the artifacts are for sale, and each item includes a fascinating history. Even antiques with unknown stories can inspire imagination and transport customers to different eras. An old dining table might be the lone remaining witness to a special family dinner on the night before the two oldest sons enlisted in the Union army and, weeks later, died in Gettysburg. The same Victorian-era mirror that helped a woman to check the alignment of her crinolette in 1870 probably reflected images of the moon-landing on a television set in the same room in 1969. Old paintings, displayed on walls for dozens of years, could have touched the lives of countless people, perhaps in ways that significantly altered lives and, thus, the future. Dealers who have built lives around these captivating antiques are now providing ways to take the experience to new levels by providing, in addition to antiques, interior decorating services.

2   A visit to the showroom of an established antiques dealer-decorator in Reading, Pennsylvania, will reveal a two-level harlequin floor covered with eighteenth-century furniture. The walls and ceiling are loaded with corresponding period accessories: chandeliers, mirrors, china, art prints, and wall hangings. A separate room contains even more period artifacts such as columns, iron gates, and modernized lighting fixtures. Adjacent rooms in the dealership contain similar arrangements with nineteenth- and twentieth-century antiques. Most of these later artifacts qualify as Americana, and many of them are very rare or very unusual; for example, there is Native American art, furniture made from recycled cigar boxes, and a full-body stuffed moose complete with antlers.

3   Despite the array of artifacts, the largest contributing factor of the dealer's success is the arrangement of the shop itself. Furniture and accessories are displayed in the same fashion that a modern furniture company would display complete suites. Not all of the items are matched in make or origin, but the dealer applies a lifetime of expertise and good taste to ensure that items match in style, color, and period. Customers can then shop for completed arrangements of antiques, and, if they want items that the dealer does not stock, the dealer will gladly offer locating services. Dealers will also provide locating services if they need to find items that match a specific interior decoration design.

4   As a logical attempt to further establish and expand business, many antiques dealers now offer interior decorating services. With decades of education through experience, antiques dealers are often the authorities in total arrangement accuracy. In addition to identifying proper furniture and accessories, dealer-decorators can recommend proper paint schemes, woodwork, masonry, carpet, and flooring to match existing homes, color schemes, and personalities. Allowing decorators to create the proper ambiance, of course, requires great

confidence on behalf of buyers, but the credentialed decorator will be able to create arrangements that glow with the aura of the selected time period. Furthermore, most reputable dealers guarantee their coordination skills with their antique furnishings, which is why they are often called upon to decorate notable venues such as period houses, inns, restaurants, and hotels. Most dealers prefer to work with genuine antiques. Reproduction antiques are available, but most dealers shun them as cheap substitutes, and it seldom poses a problem because customers who can afford such decorating services can usually afford the genuine antiques as well.

5   Antiques dealer-decorators are still dealers at heart, so collectors need not worry that individual antiques will ever become scarce or too overpriced. One unchanging aspect of antique dealerships is that they all get overcrowded with artifacts at some point, and dealers solve this problem by hosting "house sales" to make room for new collections. Many dealers rent trucks or vans and take their goods to flea markets or auctions with the intention of selling every last piece of cargo. Antiques dealers like nothing better than driving home empty trucks, so it is extremely possible to find excellent prices for what could be valuable antiques at these events. For dealers, flea markets are not just for selling antiques; at these events, dealers have the opportunity to exercise their own skills in recognizing items that would appeal to collectors. This skill ensures that dealers build effective inventories and make new customers.

6   Individual antiques can certainly be beautiful and valuable outside of a collection, but few who appreciate the intrinsic value of artifacts can quell their calling to collect more. The rewarding hobby can become quite addictive as collectors increasingly crave the craftsmanship, the distinctiveness, and even the conversational appeal that relics from past societies provide. Luckily, if collections get too large, antiques decorators can ensure that portals to previous times will be accurate, attractive places—single rooms or entire homes—in which time can stop for a while.

1. What is the error in the first sentence?
   A. *Artifacts* is too closely related to *antiques*.
   B. Fascinating is too subjective.
   C. The colon should be a semi-colon.
   D. The comma after *sale* is unnecessary.
   E. There is no error.

2. Which is the author's intention for including the descriptions of objects in paragraph 1?
   A. to inform readers about the table
   B. to convince readers to become antiques dealers
   C. to explain why antique furniture is better than new furniture
   D. to explain the mysterious appeal of antiques
   E. to foreshadow an event later in the passage

3. In paragraph 2, the word *harlequin* refers to
   A. paperback romance stories.
   B. a court jester mannequins.
   C. beetle-type bugs.
   D. old-fashion.
   E. a diamond-shaped pattern.

4. In paragraph 2, *Americana* refers to
   A. furniture made in the USA.
   B. antiques that reflect the culture of the United States.
   C. imported reproductions of American antiques.
   D. Southwest American Indian artifacts.
   E. artifacts of American architecture.

5. According to paragraph 3, why would an antiques dealer offer locating services?
   A. to find antiques of a lost period
   B. to locate more items to put in the shop
   C. to find antiques to match an interior design
   D. to complete a decorating scheme
   E. to offer a particular interior design for a certain customer

6. As used in paragraph 4, *ambiance* most nearly means
   A. behavior.
   B. furnishings.
   C. lighting.
   D. atmosphere.
   E. artwork.

7. Antiques dealers handle an overstocking of inventory by
    A. offering in-store merchandise at half price.
    B. having house sales or by selling items outside their dealerships.
    C. moving everything to a special room.
    D. selling the house.
    E. having a going-out-of-business sale.

8. It is important for dealers to educate themselves in recognizing items of interest to collectors because
    A. it shows expertise in pottery making, calligraphy, and basketry.
    B. it inspires new decorative schemes that attract customers.
    C. it gets dealers contracts with restaurants and hotels.
    D. it helps successfully date artifacts and identify forgeries.
    E. it helps to build proper inventories and to please new customers.

9. Which of the following ideas does the last sentence of the passage suggest?
    A. Restored antiques last much longer than common furniture.
    B. People will probably never perfect time travel.
    C. It is beneficial to create the effect that time has slowed or stopped.
    D. Antiques decorators manipulate time for a fee.
    E. Antiques allow people to feel what people from other times felt.

10. This passage would most likely be found in a/an
    A. encyclopedia.
    B. local business feature of a newspaper.
    C. letter to a friend.
    D. home-improvement magazine.
    E. advertising brochure.

Lesson Nineteen

1. **tantamount** (tan´ tə maunt) *adj.* of essentially equal value or significance
   To the professor, using notes during tests is *tantamount* to cheating.
   syn: equivalent; commensurate   *ant: incomparable*

2. **subversive** (səb vər´ siv) *adj.* in opposition to authority or government
   The king imprisoned the author for writing a book with *subversive* ideas.
   syn: dissident; rebellious   *ant: loyal*

3. **conducive** (kən dōō´ siv) *adj.* tending to cause or bring about
   Job dissatisfaction is often *conducive* to high levels of stress.
   syn: contributive

4. **amenable** (ə mē´ nə bəl) *adj.* agreeable; responsive to suggestion or advice
   The *amenable* boss listened to and acted upon the workers' complaints.
   syn: responsive; tractable   *ant: inflexible*

5. **stricture** (strik´ chər) *n.* a restraint or limit
   Faced with overpopulation, the government enacted harsh *strictures* on immigration.
   syn: constraints; limitations

6. **sedentary** (se´ dən ter ē) *adj.* characterized by or requiring sitting; motionless
   The regional salesman sought a *sedentary* job that did not require driving or heavy lifting every day.
   syn: inactive

7. **influx** (in´ fluks) *n.* an inward flow
   Thanks to wise investing, Meg's bank account had a steady *influx* of money.
   ant: outflow

8. **rigorous** (ri´ gə rəs) *adj.* severe; relentless; harsh
   Few people completed the *rigorous* trek to the summit of Mount Everest.
   syn: arduous; austere; grueling   *ant: easy; painless*

9. **patina** (pə tē´ nə) *n.* a sheen on a surface resulting from age and use
   The *patina* on the antique lamp gave the item character but reduced its value.

10. **placebo** (plä sē´ bō) *n.* a fake drug used in the testing of medication
    Half of the test subjects ingested the real drug, and the other half took
    placebos.

11. **junta** (hun´ tə) *n.* a military group ruling a country after seizing power
    After the revolution, a *junta* governed the island nation until elections
    were held.

12. **pinnacle** (pi´ ni kəl) *n.* a peak or climax
    The *pinnacle* of her career was her two-month trip to Russia.
    syn: summit; apex   *ant: nadir*

13. **mollify** (mä´ lə fī) *v.* to reduce, soothe, or calm
    Amber attempted to *mollify* the baby by singing her a song.
    syn: placate; pacify   *ant: enrage*

14. **perjury** (pər´ jə rē) *n.* the act of lying under oath
    A *perjury* charge added to the length of the guilty man's incarceration.

15. **plaintive** (plān´ tiv) *adj.* expressing sorrow; mournful
    The *plaintive* poem brought tears to her eyes.
    syn: melancholic   *ant: joyful*

EXERCISE I—Words in Context

*From the list below, supply the words needed to complete the paragraph. Some
words will not be used.*

influx	pinnacle	sedentary	junta
conducive	rigorous	strictures	

1. Heather knew that she would need to impose some _____ on her eat-
    ing habits in order to comply with her _____ training regimen in the
    weeks before the marathon. Timing was crucial; in order to place well,
    Heather would need to reach the _____ of her fitness on the day of
    the race. Several days of rest before the race will be _____ to her win-
    ning, but until that time, no one will regard Heather as _____; if she's
    not sleeping, she will be running.

From the list below, supply the words needed to complete the paragraph. Some words will not be used.

> perjury   rigorous   influx   plaintive
> amenable   tantamount   mollify

2. The steady _____ of observers continued until every seat in the courtroom was filled. Everyone watched the famous defendant, who appeared to be _____ as she nodded in affirmation to each whisper from her lawyer. While on the stand, the defendant had a[n] _____ look as she described the guilt that she felt for her crimes; however, during the cross-examination, the prosecutor succeeded in provoking the defendant until she lost her temper. She stood and screamed in rage.

    "Defense, please _____ your client," said the judge. After the outburst, the trial fell apart for the defense. The jury deliberated and found the defendant guilty, and one of the witnesses faced _____ charges for lying on behalf of the defendant.

From the list below, supply the words needed to complete the paragraph. Some words will not be used.

> junta   sedentary   mollify   subversive
> patina   placebo   tantamount

3. The _____ on the brass buttons of General Blanco's uniform sparkled in the sun when he stepped outside of the capital office and fished in his pockets for his pill box. Only his doctor knew that the general was about to take a[n] _____ that consisted of little more than sugar. Days before, the general had demanded treatment for recurring chest pains. The doctor found nothing wrong with the general, so he prescribed a psychological treatment for what he thought was a psychological illness.

    General Blanco's malady was likely the result of a very stressful situation. At the time the pains began, he was a member of a five-person _____ that had seized control of an impoverished nation, and plenty of _____ citizens would have liked nothing more than to eliminate the militant rulers and reinstall the exiled dictator. Blanco had had some experience _____ to leading his nation, but little experience in dodging assassins.

EXERCISE II—Sentence Completion

Complete the sentence in a way that shows you understand the meaning of the italicized vocabulary word.

1. Judging by the *patina* on the doorknob, the house...

2. The *junta* took control of the government after...

3. To some employers, taking office supplies for home use is *tantamount* to...

4. The little girl seemed *plaintive* after...

5. During the *pinnacle* of the story, the heroine...

6. The builder said that warm, damp conditions in the basement are *conducive* to...

7. *Strictures* on the number of fish you can catch are meant to...

8. Pauline's *rigorous* morning workout includes...

9. Ted was fired for *perjury* after he...

10. Some *subversive* citizens refused to acknowledge the new law that...

11. Will attributed his fast recovery to the *influx* of ...

12. The photographer required his subjects to be *sedentary* so that...

13. Half of the experimental rats received a *placebo*, while the other half received...

14. The usually *amenable* students in the class surprised the substitute teacher by...

15. The police could not *mollify* the man after he learned that...

EXERCISE III—Roots, Prefixes, and Suffixes

Study the entries and answer the questions that follow.

The root *phon* means "sound."
The prefix *tele* means "afar" or "at a distance."
The root *put* means "to clean," "to prune," or "to reckon."

1. Using literal translations as guidance, define the following words without using a dictionary.

    A. telephone D. television
    B. repute   E. compute
    C. polyphony F. symphonic

2. A battlefield surgeon might want to _____ someone's infected limb, but someone who does not think that the operation is necessary might _____ the doctor's decision.

3. List as many words as you can think of that contain the roots *phon* or *put*.

EXERCISE IV—Inference

Complete the sentences by inferring information about the italicized word from its context.

1. If someone is as *sedentary* as a statue, then that person is...

2. A store might choose an *amenable* person to work in the complaint department because he or she will...

3. If inhalation of asbestos is *conducive* to developing lung cancer, people who work in asbestos mines should...

EXERCISE V—Writing

Here is a writing prompt similar to the one you will find on the writing portion of the SAT.

Plan and write an essay based on the following statement:

There is nothing so horrible as languid study; when you sit looking at the clock, wishing the time was over, or that somebody would call on you and put you out of your misery. The only way to read with any efficacy, is to read so heartily, that dinnertime comes two hours before you expected it.

–Sydney Smith (1771-1845)
"How to Read"

Assignment: In an essay, explain what Sydney Smith means by "languid study" and discuss the practicality of his suggested remedy for the condition. Support your position with evidence from your reading, classroom studies, experience, and observation.

Thesis: Write a one-sentence response to the assignment. Make certain this single sentence offers a clear statement of your position.

Example: Sydney Smith properly advises readers to become entirely absorbed by the material, and it will make the reading a much more enjoyable experience.

Organizational Plan: If your thesis is the point on which you want to end, where does your essay need to begin? List the points of development that are inevitable in leading your reader from your beginning point to your end point. This list is your outline.

Draft: Use your thesis as both your beginning and your end. Following your outline, write a good first draft of your essay. Remember to support all your points with examples, facts, references to reading, etc.

Review and Revise: Exchange essays with a classmate. Using the Holistic scoring guide on page 225, score your partner's essay (while he or she scores yours). Focus on the development of ideas and use of language conventions. If necessary, rewrite your essay to correct the problems indicated by the essay's score.

Improving Paragraphs

Read the following passage and then answer the multiple-choice questions that follow. The questions will require you to make decisions regarding the revision of the reading selection.

(1) Clothes hangers are one of mankind's greatest peeves because they are a necessary evil. (2) The way in which the simple creatures complicate daily life reveals their satanic inclination. (3) Wire hangers are the worst; it is rumored that they exist solely to irritate the user. (4) At night, while humans sleep, wire hangers converse about how they can collectively infuriate people who try to remove hangers from their natural state—the puzzle-like entanglement. (5) Inseparable, the hangers devise ways to best fuse themselves to one another by interweaving their long, thin arms and necks.

(6) Sadly, humans appear to be years away from solving the coat hanger dilemma. (7) Even in this age of space exploration, digital information, and quantum physics, we can find no better way to hang clothing than with hangers. (8) We try hooks, which work fairly well, but they leave permanent divots in garments in the spot on which the garment was hanged. (9) A garment hung by the sleeve, for example, looks rather strange when worn with a pointy bulge emanating from the shoulder.

(10) Wood hangers only prove to be greater foes than their wire cousins. (11) They are weighty and bulky, and when they're not used to hang heavy overcoats, they usurp all available space in the closet. (12) When wood hangers are not taking up precious space, they are trying to escape; their most common method is to grab any adjacent wire hanger as it is picked from the rack. (13) Plastic hangers, while mildly friendlier than wooden hangers, have their own annoying idiosyncrasies, the first being the tiny hook-like appendages that are allegedly for securing the hanging loops of skirts. (14) These little hooks were obviously engineered by clothing manufacturers because they invariably break off and leave sharp edges to fray the inside of the blouse that accompanies the skirt. (15) It's cruel, indeed, but to make things worse, skirts actually hung by their loops develop distinct creases that make re-ironing necessary. (16) Re-ironing is the ultimate goal of any hanger separated from its nest.

(17) One particularly devilish species of hanger is the one with the white cardboard roll on the bottom for hanging slacks without producing a fold mark. (18) These hangers, while not quite as cunning as plastic hangers, are perhaps the most treacherous because they don't even try to function as they are designed. (19) Immediately after placing a load upon the hanger, however minuscule, the cardboard tube collapses into its natural equilibrium—the classic V-shape. (20) The more astute cardboard-roll hangers wait until they have been placed in the closet, out of view, before they collapse. (21) This ensures that they carry out that prime directive of all hangers—to render the clothing wrinkled and unfit for wearing in public.

(22) No one knows what the future holds for the human hanger dilemma, but certainly scientists are working around the clock to remedy the blight. (23) Until that solution arrives, we must stay one step ahead of the hangers. (24) We must retaliate and deny their happiness. (25) Ridicule the hanger, and then show it that you're in charge by simply throwing the clothes on the floor and wrinkling them yourself. (26) The next time that you are about to detangle a hanger, stop.

1. Which of the following suggestions would improve the introduction of the passage?
    A. Start paragraph 1 with sentence 4.
    B. Start a new paragraph with sentence 5.
    C. Start paragraph 1 aith sentence 6.
    D. Start a new paragraph after sentence 2.
    E. Start a new paragraph after sentence 3.

2. Which of the following corrects a usage error in paragraph 2?
    A. Hyphenate *quantum physics*.
    B. Change *hanged* to *hung*.
    C. Capitalize *age*.
    D. Correct the spelling of *garment*.
    E. Insert a semicolon after *physics*.

3. Which change to the paragraph sequence would improve the organization of the passage?
    A. Exchange paragraph 1 with paragraph 3.
    B. Exchange paragraph 2 with paragraph 3.
    C. Move paragraph 2 so it follows paragraph 4.
    D. Delete paragraph 2.
    E. Delete paragraph 3.

4. Which of the following would best improve paragraph 3?
    A. Begin a new paragraph after sentence 10.
    B. Begin a new paragraph after sentence 11.
    C. Begin a new paragraph after sentence 12.
    D. Begin a new paragraph after sentence 13.
    E. Begin a new paragraph after sentence 14.

5. Which of the following best clarifies paragraph 5?
    A. Exchange sentence 22 with sentence 23.
    B. Exchange sentence 25 with sentence 26.
    C. Exchange sentence 24 with sentence 25.
    D. Delete sentence 26.
    E. Make two sentences from sentence 22.

Lesson Twenty

1. **impasse** (im´ pas) *n.* a problem or predicament with no obvious
      resolution
   Fighting resumed when the two factions reached an *impasse* during the
   peace talks.
   syn: gridlock; stalemate; standoff

2. **wunderkind** (vun´ dər kint) *n.* one who excels in a difficult field at
      an early age
   The ten-year-old *wunderkind* mastered organic chemistry while his peers
   learned the basics of long division.
   syn: prodigy

3. **acumen** (ə kyü´ mən) *n.* ability to discern or discriminate;
      shrewdness
   Hal's business *acumen* made him an excellent stock broker.
   syn: keenness; sharpness　　　　　　　　*ant: ignorance; naiveté*

4. **nanotechnology** (na nō tek nä´ lə jē) *n.* the use of single atoms and
      molecules to construct microscopic devices
   Scientists hope to use *nanotechnology* to create tiny robots that can be
   injected into the body to destroy cancer cells.

5. **notarize** (nō´ tə rīz) *v.* to certify legally
   Someone will *notarize* the signatures on the title to complete the sale of
   a car.

6. **piquant** (pē´ känt) *adj.* a strong, stimulating taste
   A mix of herbs and spices gave Joe's chili a *piquant* taste.
   syn: spicy; tangy　　　　　　　　*ant: bland*

7. **malodorous** (mal ō´ də rəs) *adj.* having an offensive odor
   People ten miles away could smell the *malodorous* chicken processing
   plant.
   syn: stinking

8. **pungent** (pən´ jənt) *adj.* a sharp taste; acrid
   The dairy store offered samples of both mild and *pungent* types of
   cheeses.
   syn: sharp　　　　　　　　*ant: mild*

9. **erroneous** (i rō´ nē əs) *adj.* incorrect; mistaken
    Read the questions carefully, or you'll have *erroneous* answers on the test.
    syn: flawed   *ant: correct*

10. **concurrent** (kən kər´ ənt) *adj.* happening at the same time
    This year, Jane's birthday happens to be *concurrent* with Easter.
    syn: simultaneous   *ant: conflicting; separate*

11. **negligible** (ne´ gli jə bəl) *adj.* of little importance; insignificant
    The car was in great shape except for a few *negligible* scratches.
    syn: unimportant; trifling   *ant: significant; noteworthy*

12. **renege** (ri nig´) *v.* to break a promise or obligation; revoke
    Pete *reneged* on his promise to care for his dog, so his parents gave the
    animal away.
    syn: breach; abandon

13. **precept** (prē´ sept) *n.* a rule of action; a principle to live by
    Kim lived by the *precepts* of modesty, courtesy, and moderation.
    syn: law; axiom

14. **visage** (vi´ zij) *n.* a face or facial expression
    Ken's *visage* turned to anger when he saw the neighbor's dog in his own
    swimming pool.
    syn: countenance; features

15. **irrevocable** (i re´ və kə bəl) *adj.* impossible to retract or revoke;
        irreversible
    The decision to divorce was *irrevocable*.
    syn: permanent; unchangeable

EXERCISE I—Words in Context

*From the list below, supply the words needed to complete the paragraph. Some
words will not be used.*

renege	precept	pungent	notarize
negligible	acumen	visage	erroneous

1. Dave could not help noticing Daria's furious _____ as she pulled her
    sputtering car into his driveway. She parked the car and stomped across the
    lawn until she found Dave sitting on the porch.
       "I want my money back," said Daria. "I've had the car for only an hour,
    so it shouldn't be a problem for you to return the money. This whole
    episode has left a[n] _____, ugly taste in my mouth."
       "I'm afraid that your assumption is _____," said Dave in a smug
    tone. "The clerk _____ the sales contract; you bought the car 'as-is,'
    and the transaction is official. You can't _____ on the deal at this
    point. Besides, it's not my fault that you didn't have the _____ to real-
    ize that the car is a piece of junk." Daria made fists, grumbled, and stormed
    back to the lemon that she had just purchased.

*From the list below, supply the words needed to complete the paragraph. Some
words will not be used.*

nanotechnology	precept	pungent	wunderkind
irrevocable	impasse	concurrent	

2. "Every word is recorded in this laboratory, so use caution because anything
    you say will be _____," Dr. Bryant warned Matt as they walked past
    the _____ department of the robotics research division. Matt was still
    ecstatic about his new job with Neutrodyne, a world leader in robotic tech-
    nology. Like many of the research staff, Matt had been a[n] _____
    who had completed high school and college by the age of seventeen. Now,
    at twenty-six, he had a doctorate in physics and was the first choice for
    recruiters from several major corporations, three of which were govern-
    ment contractors. Matt had decided to take the job with Neutrodyne
    because he was afraid that he might reach a[n] _____ working for the
    government if his political views did not support the nature of his assigned
    research. He wanted the ability to merge his _____ with his career,
    and Neutrodyne seemed to be the best place to do it.

From the list below, supply the words needed to complete the paragraph. Some words will not be used.

malodorous	negligible	impasse	piquant
concurrent	acumen		

3.   Since the Soup Olympics and the Champion Cookoff were _____ this year, Kevin had to make two separate batches of his famous seafood bisque. He stayed up all night before the contests, stirring and adding tiny amounts of _____ spices until he felt that the soup was perfect. To an inexperienced taster, Kevin's tiny additions produced _____ changes in the food, but to the judges, Kevin knew, the tiny differences would determine who won and who lost. If the bisque lacked in one particular spice, or if the judge detected the faintest _____ scent from the sample, Kevin would forfeit first prize.

EXERCISE II—Sentence Completion

Complete the sentence in a way that shows you understand the meaning of the italicized vocabulary word.

1. If Dianne had known that her decision was going to be *irrevocable*, she...

2. Since the flood was *concurrent* with the earthquake, the damage...

3. If no one *notarizes* the contract, it will...

4. After fleeing the police, the mugger found himself at an *impasse* when he...

5. Norman's youthful *visage* disappeared after...

6. The back parking lot was *malodorous* in the summer because...

7. At only six years of age, the *wunderkind* could...

8. Brad's parents were confident that their son had the *precepts* to...

9. To give the bread a *pungent* flavor, the cook...

10. The expert in *nanotechnology* lectured the students on...

11. Paul *reneged* on his dinner plans when he found out...

12. One *erroneous* entry in the database will cause...

13. Lovers of *piquant* food came from miles around to try...

14. Rhonda told the pizza-delivery man to keep the *negligible* amount of...

15. Teri's *acumen* in identifying personality types made her good at...

EXERCISE III—Roots, Prefixes, and Suffixes

Study the entries and answer the questions that follow.

The prefixes *ambi* and *amphi* mean "both" or "around."
The roots *luc* and *lum* mean "light."
The prefix *super* means "above" or "over."
The root *magn* means "great."

1. Using literal translations as guidance, define the following words without using a dictionary.

   A. luminary   D. magnitude
   B. translucent   E. magnate
   C. amphibious   F. superintendent

2. Someone who can use both hands equally well is called _____. An *ambiguous* statement can be interpreted in _____.

3. You might use a lamp to _____ your desktop so that you can see your work. If the filament in the light bulb does not become _____, you will know that the bulb is burned out.

4. List as many words as you can think of that contain the root *magn* or the prefix *super*.

EXERCISE IV—Inference

Complete the sentences by inferring information about the italicized word from its context.

1. If you *renege* on a deal once, few people will...

2. Sports stars and team owners might reach an *impasse* about contracts if...

3. One good *precept* to remember throughout your life is...

EXERCISE V—Critical Reading

Below is a pair of reading passages followed by several multiple-choice questions similar to the ones you will encounter on the SAT. Carefully read both passages and choose the best answer to each of the questions.

The authors of the following passages focus on Halloween. Both of the passages contain information about the origins of Halloween, but they focus on the event in different historical periods.

Passage 1

Lots of people celebrate Halloween, but only a few realize that the origins of the autumn celebration rest in ancient history. The predominant theory about the origins of Halloween is that the celebration descended from the ancient Celtic festival of Samhain.

5   For the Celts living in Ireland and northern England during the fifth century B.C., Samhain was the most important festival of the year. Celebrated on the first of November, Samhain honored the end of the year and marked the beginning of the new year. For the Celts, November was a logical time to observe the new year; November marked the end of the harvest season, and it heralded the

10   onset of winter, a potentially deadly season for early cultures. It was only appropriate that the unstoppable winter, whose biting cold and long dark nights drained the life from both crops and people, was a symbol of death. On the eve of the Celtic New Year—the night that we now call Halloween—the Celts believed that a doorway to the spirit world opened, and that the spirits of those

15   who died throughout the year were free to once again roam the world of the living. During the eve of the new year, the Celts wore costumes while priests conducted rituals around sacrificial pyres.

The beliefs and traditions associated with Samhain slowly changed in the centuries following the peak of Celtic civilization. Romans conquered most of

20   the Celtic lands and had incorporated some of their own beliefs into the Samhain festivities by A.D. 100. After Christianity had spread to Celtic lands by the eighth century, the day of the Celtic New Year became All-hallows, a day of honoring Christian saints. We now refer to the eve of November first as All-hallows Eve, or Halloween; despite cultural shifts, however, the descendents of the Celts

25   never quite abandoned the ancient belief that spirits roamed the earth on Halloween. People augmented the old Celtic beliefs with new legends, the most notable of which was perhaps the legend that spirits not only roamed the earth, but that they also sought new bodies to possess.

Wary of spirit possession, the Celtic descendents had to develop adequate

30   defenses, the first of which was disguise. Having assumed that spirits would ignore their own kind, people disguised themselves as spirits if they ventured outdoors on Halloween. As a second precaution, people placed offerings of food on their doorsteps; they hoped that any evil spirits roaming the night would be

35 satisfied with the food and decline to enter the homes. People who left no treat
for the spirits, of course, risked provoking the wandering spirits and rendering
themselves prone to tricks.

Few of the modern Halloween revelers stop to think about the historic roots
of the holiday. Many people incorrectly assume that the holiday symbolizes an
assemblage of evil rituals or devil worship, and that is certainly not the case.
40 While the Celts did perhaps believe that spirits roamed the earth on the eve of
the new year, the traditions that they established were innocent and festive, just
as they are today.

Passage 2

Few holidays spark the interests and imaginations of children as well as
Halloween. For nearly a century, Americans have embraced the tradition of decorating homes with the fruits of harvest and donning costumes in an effort to
ward off evil spirits and, maybe, scare a few treats out of neighbors.

5 The Halloween that we know did not come into practice until the late nineteenth century. Long dormant in America, the celebration experienced resur-
gence when the influx of Irish and Scottish immigrants brought old Celtic traditions to North America. Americans began dressing up in costumes and, in mer-
riment, went from house to house asking for food. People who offered no food
10 were prone to tricks—good-humored "punishments" for their lack of hospitality.

As poverty increased around the turn of the century, young urbanites began
to taint the benevolent spirit of Halloween. What were once benign tricks slowly
became acts of vandalism that only detracted from the autumn festivities.
Fearing that such behavior might destroy an enjoyable tradition, people planned
15 ways to turn Halloween into a community event.

Shortly after the turn of the century, communities organized block parties,
dances, and other Halloween festivities that brought people together and, at the
same time, discouraged the destructive activities of wayward pranksters. People
were encouraged to offer small treats as a way to rekindle the festive nature of
20 Halloween and to curb vandalism. This was the birth of the still-popular
American Halloween tradition.

While a very small minority claims Halloween for a time to celebrate the
wicked, Halloween for the majority is a time of innocent festivity, when families
can spend time together and children can explore the limits of their creativity.
25 Controversy will always surround the jovial season and the way in which it is
celebrated, but Halloween will always be a source of fun childhood memories
and a way to celebrate, or even parody, our fears of the unknown.

1.   The original Celts, according to passage 1, observed Samhain around
     which of the following time periods?
     A.   1941-1945 B.C.
     B.   400-500 B.C.
     C.   A.D. 100-200
     D.   A.D. 700-800
     E.   The Celts still observe Samhain.

2.   According to the first passage, the ancient Celts celebrated Samhain for
     the same reason that modern people might celebrate
     A.   President's Day.
     B.   Boxing Day.
     C.   Halloween.
     D.   New Year.
     E.   Valentine's Day.

3.   According to the first passage, winter was an appropriate symbol of death
     because
     A.   it killed food supplies.
     B.   it caused people to freeze.
     C.   it caused the death of animals.
     D.   it caused the death of plants and people.
     E.   it slowed the movement of the spirits.

4.   Descendents of the Celts thought that disguises would protect them from
     spirits because
     A.   the ancient Celts wore costumes and lived through Halloween.
     B.   they thought that spirits would not bother other spirits.
     C.   they thought that the spirits would not be able to find them.
     D.   spirits could not stand the way that Celts looked.
     E.   wearing disguises was a part of the New Year tradition.

5.   In line 26 of the first passage, the word *augmented* most nearly means
     A.   supplemented.
     B.   rewrote.
     C.   abolished.
     D.   imitated.
     E.   believed.

6. The intention of the first passage is to
    A. persuade that Halloween is not evil.
    B. inform how Halloween influenced the rituals of Samhain.
    C. develop an argument against Halloween.
    D. inform about the early roots of Halloween traditions.
    E. instruct readers on how to emulate the ancient Celts.

7. According to the second passage, Halloween tricks were originally
    A. scornful songs that trick-or-treaters sang when they were not satisfied with their treats.
    B. ways for spirits to enter homes.
    C. severe punishments imposed on people who offered no food.
    D. a way to limit vandalism.
    E. harmless tricks played on people who provided no treats.

8. According to the second passage, which best describes why Halloween was threatened during the turn of the century?
    A. Poverty increased.
    B. Celtic people abandoned their traditions.
    C. Block parties were not yet invented.
    D. Children had discipline problems.
    E. Vandalism increased during Halloween.

9. As used in line 12 of the second passage, *benign* most nearly means
    A. harmless.
    B. expensive.
    C. legendary.
    D. illogical.
    E. careless.

10. The authors of both passages would probably agree that
    A. Halloween is detrimental to children.
    B. Halloween should be practiced like Samhain.
    C. Halloween is an inoffensive, festive celebration.
    D. Samhain should be illegal.
    E. modern practices are nearly perfect imitations of the ancient Celtic rituals.

11.   The two passages differ most in
      A.   tone, because the first is argumentative while the second is strictly informative.
      B.   topic, because the first informs about ancient history while the second informs about modern history.
      C.   subject, because the first informs about Celts while the second informs about Halloween.
      D.   setting, because they take place in different areas of the world.
      E.   characters, because the Romans are not mentioned in the second passage.

12.   The most appropriate title for either of the passages is
      A.   America's Favorite Holiday.
      B.   Ancient Halloween.
      C.   Modern Halloween.
      D.   The History of Halloween.
      E.   The Many Aspects of Halloween.

Lesson Twenty-One

1. **confute** (kən fyo͞ot´) *v.* to argue or point out error
   The candidate *confuted* every aspect of his opponent's proposed policies.
   syn: refute; disprove   *ant: confirm; verify*

2. **meritorious** (mer ə tôr´ ē əs) *adj.* deserving of an award or honor
   The young corporal won a medal for his *meritorious* actions in combat.
   syn: commendable; laudable; praiseworthy   *ant: despicable; unworthy*

3. **mezzanine** (mez ə nēn´) *n.* the lowest balcony in a theater; a partial
   story between main stories in a building
   Kelly had an excellent view of the show from her seat in the *mezzanine.*

4. **tribulation** (tri byə lā´ shən) *n.* an affliction, trouble, or difficult
   experience
   The death of Betty's father was a time of *tribulation* for the entire family.
   syn: ordeal; hardship

5. **recumbent** (ri kəm´ bənt) *adj.* resting or lying down
   The *recumbent* children soon fell asleep.
   syn: reclining   *ant: upright*

6. **dynasty** (dī´ nəs tē) *n.* a succession of rulers from the same family or
   group
   The Romanov *dynasty* ruled Russia for more than 300 years.

7. **purport** (pər pôrt´) *v.* to claim; to have or to give the false impression
   of being
   The newspaper *purports* to be objective, but it is actually very biased in
   its reporting.
   syn: allege; claim; maintain

8. **forte** (fôrt, fôr´ tā) *n.* an area of expertise or strength
   Jane is good at mathematics, but science is her *forte.*
   syn: specialty; talent   *ant: weakness*

9. **kleptomania** (klep tə mān´ ē ə) *n.* a continual urge to steal regardless
   of economic motive
   Unable to control her *kleptomania,* the wealthy actress shoplifted a pair
   of shoes.

10. **renown**   (ri noun´)   *n.*   state of being well known and honored; fame
The actor enjoyed world *renown* after starring in a blockbuster film.
syn: notoriety; popularity   *ant: anonymity; obscurity*

11. **ineffable**   (i ne´ fə bəl)   *adj.*   too sacred or great to be described; indescribable
Lynn could not believe the *ineffable* beauty of the mountains in the distance.
syn: inexpressible; unspeakable

12. **fortitude**   (for´ tə tŏŏd)   *n.*   strength in adversity
If not for the *fortitude* of the soldiers on the front line, we would have lost the battle.
syn: determination; tenacity   *ant: weakness*

13. **botch**   (bätch)   *v.*   to ruin through clumsiness; to bungle
Bill *botched* the experiment when he forgot to water the plants.
                                                        ant: fix

14. **perennial**   (pə ren´ ē əl)   *adj.*   lasting indefinitely
The parents tried to instill a *perennial* feeling of worth in their child.
syn: enduring; perpetual   *ant: fleeting; limited*

15. **brinkmanship**   (brink´ mən ship)   *n.*   pushing dangerous situations to the edge of disaster rather than conceding
President Kennedy's blockade during the Cuban Missile Crisis could have led to nuclear war, but this act of *brinkmanship* ended with the peaceful removal of weapons.

EXERCISE I—Words in Context

From the list below, supply the words needed to complete the paragraph. Some words will not be used.

renown	forte	confute	brinkmanship
dynasty	recumbent	tribulation	

1. Damian mounted his new _____ bicycle, but he immediately crashed into a light pole because he was not used to sitting back while riding a bike. After a few minutes of _____, though, he was able to ride around in the parking lot without falling down. Damian's friends _____ his decision to spend a lot of money on what they called a novelty item, but Damian was _____ for wasting money on things that sat in the basement and collected dust when he tired of them. His credit card sprees would stop eventually. Damian was bound to lose his game of financial _____, in which he waited to pay his bills until he received threatening notices from the bank.

From the list below, supply the words needed to complete the paragraph. Some words will not be used.

fortitude	perennial	recumbent	purport
forte	botch	meritorious	

2. Mohandas Gandhi never _____ himself to be a great leader, and his _____ was certainly not his public speaking ability. Nonetheless, Gandhi's _____ service to his people brought independence to India, and his _____ message, that any nation willing to unite in patience and _____ can overcome its oppressors, will be remembered forever.

From the list below, supply the words needed to complete the paragraph. Some words will not be used.

mezzanine	dynasty	tribulation	kleptomania
botch	meritorious	ineffable	

3. During preparation for his twenty-first burglary, Simon wondered if, perhaps, he suffered from a type of _____. He had already amassed a small fortune from the sale of stolen art, but he always seemed to need to pull off "just one more job" before he retired permanently. He almost retired involuntarily when he _____ the last job by dropping a statuette of _____ beauty from the _____ of the art museum while fumbling with his night vision goggles. The relic, which dated back to the Ming _____, shattered when it struck the floor far below.

EXERCISE II—Sentence Completion

Complete the sentence in a way that shows you understand the meaning of the italicized vocabulary word.

1. Jake planned to spend his afternoon *recumbent* in…

2. Judy longed for the life of *renown* that only…

3. I *confuted* the question on the test because it…

4. From the *mezzanine* in the factory, the foreman shouted…

5. If math is not your *forte*, then you should…

6. Davy *botched* the car's paint job when he…

7. The hostage crisis turned into a dangerous game of *brinkmanship* when the criminal threatened to…

8. The school honored Nicole's *meritorious* academic achievements by…

9. It is important for citizens to maintain their *fortitude* during…

10. Unless you have some form of *kleptomania*, there's no reason for you…

11. In a few minutes, the *tribulation* of learning how to swim was over and Clarence was able to…

12. For two hundred years, the *dynasty*…

13. The man *purports* to be an expert, but really he…

14. The *ineffable* sight of the Earth from the spacecraft caused…

15. April hoped to find *perennial* happiness by…

EXERCISE III—Roots, Prefixes, and Suffixes

Study the entries and answer the questions that follow.

The roots *doc* and *doct* mean "to teach" or "to cause."
The roots *au* and *esthe* mean "to feel," "to perceive," or "to hear."
The roots *cad* and *cas* mean "to fall" or "to die."

1.   Using literal translations as guidance, define the following words without using a dictionary.

     A.   document   D.   audition
     B.   auditorium   E.   anesthetize
     C.   cadence   F.   aesthetic

2.   The word _____ literally translates to "teacher," and a _____ student is easy to teach.

3.   A _____ is a dead or fallen soldier, and medical students practice their surgical techniques on *cadavers*, which are _____.

4.   List as many words as you can think of that contain the root *au*.

EXERCISE IV—Inference

Complete the sentences by inferring information about the italicized word from its context. .

1.   If you continue to *confute* the boss in front of the other workers, you might...

2.   For her *meritorious* actions that saved two lives, the lifeguard was...

3.   Because he was *recumbent* in his hammock, Pete did not...

EXERCISE V—Writing

Here is a writing prompt similar to the one you will find on the writing portion of the SAT.

> Plan and write an essay based on the following statement:
>
> It irritates me to be told how things have always been done…I
> defy the tyranny of precedent.
> > —Clara Barton (1821-1912)

Assignment: Write an essay in which you explain what Clara Barton meant by the phrase, "tyranny of precedent." Support or refute her view. Support your argument with evidence from your reading, classroom studies, experience, and observation.

Thesis: Write a one-sentence response to the assignment. Make certain this single sentence offers a clear statement of your position.

> *Example: Clara Barton's advocacy of defying precedents, or established values, is not always an effective course of action.*

Organizational Plan: If your thesis is the point on which you want to end, where does your essay need to begin? List the points of development that are inevitable in leading your reader from your beginning point to your end point. This list is your outline.

Draft: Use your thesis as both your beginning and your end. Following your outline, write a good first draft of your essay. Remember to support all your points with examples, facts, references to reading, etc.

Review and Revise: Exchange essays with a classmate. Using the Holistic scoring guide on page 225, score your partner's essay (while her or she scores yours). If necessary, rewrite your essay to correct the problems noted by your partner.

Identifying Sentence Errors

Identify the grammatical error in each of the following sentences. If the sentence contains no error, select answer choice E.

1. <u>When</u> people buy cell phones, <u>you should</u> be able <u>to afford</u> the
    (A)   (B)   (C)
    <u>roaming charges.</u>   <u>No error</u>
       (D)   (E)

2. The psychiatrist <u>found Marguerite</u> <u>to have no</u> self-confidence
                          (A)   (B)
    <u>in herself</u> <u>whatsoever.</u>   <u>No error</u>
       (C)   (D)   (E)

3. <u>We thought it was bazaar</u> to see <u>Marvin wear his</u> toupee
              (A)   (B)
    <u>backwards,</u> but he <u>seemed to think</u> it was cute.   <u>No error</u>
        (C)   (D)   (E)

4. The next time <u>that you go</u> to the <u>office store</u>, I would like you
                      (A)   (B)
    <u>to get</u> me these <u>kind</u> of pens.   <u>No error</u>
      (C)   (D)   (E)

5. If Bob <u>had begun</u> the inspection <u>earlier</u>, he <u>would have</u> completed
               (A)   (B)   (C)
    the required repairs before the <u>general's</u> visit.   <u>No error</u>
                                        (D)   (E)

Improving Sentences

The underlined portion of each sentence below contains some flaw. Select the answer choice that best corrects the flaw.

6. <u>His new pinstriped suit was worn by him</u> to the last dance of the school year.
    A. He wore a pinstriped suit
    B. His pinstriped suit, new, was worn
    C. He wore his new pinstriped suit
    D. His worn pinstriped suit he wore
    E. The new pinstriped suit was worn by him

7. Pat based the decision for his testimony on the old proverb that <u>honesty was the best policy.</u>
    A. honesty is the best policy.
    B. honesty was never the best policy.
    C. that honesty was the best policy.
    D. honesty is not always the best policy.
    E. honesty was a good policy.

8. Teachers have shown that children have a keener aptitude <u>for learning than an adult.</u>
    A. for learning than an adult has.
    B. for adult-level learning.
    C. than an adult has for learning.
    D. for learning than an adult as shown by teachers.
    E. for learning than adults.

9. <u>We had an upright piano built for a student with a transparent front.</u>
    A. We had an upright piano built with a transparent front for a student.
    B. We had an upright piano with a transparent front built for a student.
    C. We had a student upright piano with transparent front built.
    D. An upright piano built for a student had a transparent front and we had it.
    E. We had a transparent front upright piano that was built for a student.

10. <u>Don't expect Harold, Mimi, and I</u> to arrive promptly at an early morning meeting.
    A. Don't expect Harold, Mimi, and me
    B. Harold, Mimi, and me should not be expected
    C. Don't expect a meeting with Harold, Mimi, and I
    D. Harold, Mimi and I cannot be expected
    E. Don't expect Mimi, I, and Harold

REVIEW

Lessons 15 – 21

EXERCISE I – Sentence Completion

Choose the best pair of words to complete the sentence. Most choices will fit grammatically and will even make sense logically, but you must choose the pair that best fits the idea of the sentence.

Note that these words are not taken directly from lessons in this book. This exercise is intended to replicate the sentence completion portion of the SAT.

1. The _____ juvenile had been arrested twelve times before he reached eighteen, but he had not served any time in jail because of his _____.
    A. violent, tendencies
    B. incorrigible, age
    C. young, lawyers
    D. illegal, promises
    E. worst, youthfulness

2. In _____ competition, good communication between rider and horse is _____.
    A. Olympic, important
    B. riding, clear
    C. show, interesting
    D. equestrian, paramount
    E. Western, superfluous

3. Many _____ of Shakespeare were well regarded at the time, but few modern readers are _____ that they approach the Bard's genius.
    A. writers, assuaged
    B. critics, assured
    C. performers, satisfied
    D. contemporaries, convinced
    E. ideologues, ridiculed

4. Volunteering for dangerous jobs in public service increased after the ruinous conflagration, led by the _____ example of _____ from neighboring states.
   A. unselfish, firefighters
   B. precarious, police
   C. amazing, volunteers
   D. sterling, neighbors
   E. surprising, reciprocation

5. Before Columbus, scientists in ancient lands knew the world was round, but _____ prevented them from revealing this to the masses, believing the _____ would cause an abandonment of the Church teachings.
   A. modesty, truth
   B. experiments, honesty
   C. governments, revelation
   D. beliefs, anxieties
   E. superstition, curiosity

6. In order to balance the _____ of the community and the possible revenue brought in by taxes, the local government hired _____ experts.
   A. exigencies, overflow
   B. needs, efficiency
   C. desires, economic
   D. situation, professional
   E. growth, city

7. In the _____ areas of the deep oceans dwell creatures whose lives and anatomy are so otherworldly that they defy _____ belief.
   A. bottomless, clear
   B. darkened, scientific
   C. empty, all
   D. competitive, normal
   E. abyssal, rational

8. The President issued a[n] _____ to the Congress: either provide the money for his proposed _____, or he would veto any bill that came to him.
   A. ultimatum, legislation
   B. provocation, authorization
   C. threat, challenge
   D. proclamation, bill
   E. order, initiative

EXERCISE II – Crossword Puzzle

Use the clues to complete the crossword puzzle. The answers consist of vocabulary words from lessons 15 through 21.

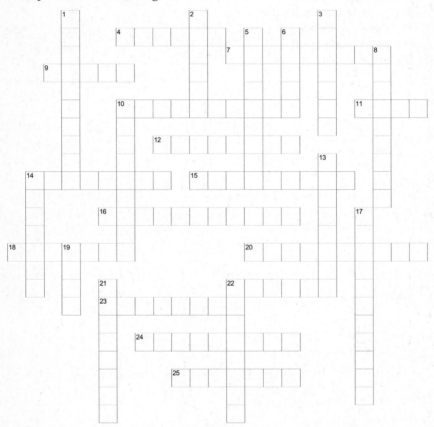

Across
4. ability to discern; shrewdness
7. schoolteacher
9. reserved; distant
10. in opposition to authority
11. prejudiced view; a preference
12. to make less severe
14. peak or climax
15. strength in adversity
16. basic; not refined
18. to argue or point out error
20. of little importance; insignificant
22. social outcast
23. to distribute or allot
24. tending to cause or bring about
25. problem with no obvious resolution

Down
1. anything causing great suffering
2. to break a promise
3. offspring; children
5. beggar
6. a concealed store of goods
8. ambiguous; intentionally vague
10. restraint or limit
13. to warn; to caution in counsel
14. to claim
17. difficult experience
19. artificial
21. absurd; ridiculously clumsy
22. strong liking

Scoring Guide for the SAT Writing Test

ORGANIZATION

6 = Clearly Competent
The paper is clearly **organized** around the central point or main idea.
The work is **free of surface errors** (grammar, spelling, punctuation, etc.).

5 = Reasonably Competent
The **organizational plan** of the paper is **clear, but not fully implemented.**
Minor surface errors are present, but they **do not interfere** with the reader's understanding of the work.

4 = Adequately Competent
The **organizational plan** of the paper is **apparent, but not consistently implemented.**
Surface errors are present, but they **do not severely interfere** with the reader's understanding.

3 = Nearly Competent
There is evidence of an **organizational plan.**
Surface errors are **apparent** and **begin to interfere** with the reader's understanding of the work.

2 = Marginally Incompetent
The **organizational plan** of the writing is obscured by **too few** details and/or **irrelevant** details.
Surface errors are **frequent and severe enough** to interfere with the reader's understanding of the work.

1 = Incompetent
There is **no clear organizational plan** and/or **insufficient material.**
Surface errors are **frequent** and **extreme**, and **severely interfere** with the reader's understanding of the work.

Scoring Guide for the SAT Writing Test

DEVELOPMENT

6 = Clearly Competent

There is **sufficient** material (details, examples, anecdotes, supporting facts, etc.) to allow the reader to feel he/she has read a full and complete discussion without notable gaps, unanswered questions, or unexplored territory in the topic. Every word, phrase, clause, and sentence is **relevant**, contributing effectively to the thesis.

The work is **free of surface errors** (grammar, spelling, punctuation, etc.).

5 = Reasonably Competent

There is **nearly sufficient** material for a full and complete discussion, but the reader is left with **a few unanswered questions**. There is no superfluous or **irrelevant** material.

Minor surface errors are present, but they **do not interfere** with the reader's understanding of the work.

4 = Adequately Competent

There is **nearly sufficient** material for a full and complete discussion, but the reader is left with **a few unanswered questions**. Irrelevant material is present.

Surface errors are present, but they **do not severely interfere** with the reader's understanding.

3 = Nearly Competent

There is evidence of an organizational plan. There are **too few** details, examples, anecdotes, supporting facts, etc.

Surface errors are **apparent** and **begin to interfere** with the reader's understanding of the work.

2 = Marginally Incompetent

The organizational plan of the writing is obscured by **too few** details and/or **irrelevant** details.

Surface errors are **frequent and severe enough** to **interfere** with the reader's understanding of the work.

1 = Incompetent

The writing sample **attempts** to discuss the topic but is **severely marred** because surface errors are **frequent** and **extreme**, and **severely interfere** with the reader's understanding of the work.

Scoring Guide for the SAT Writing Test

SENTENCE FORMATION AND VARIETY

6 = Clearly Competent
Sentences are **complete, grammatically correct**, and assist the reader in following the flow of the discussion. The use of a **variety** of sentence structures contributes to the effective organization of the work and the reader's understanding.
The work is **free of surface errors** (grammar, spelling, punctuation, etc.).

5 = Reasonably Competent
Sentences are **complete, generally correct,** and do not distract the reader from the flow of the discussion. There is evidence of a concerted effort to use a **variety** of structures.
Minor surface errors are present, but they **do not interfere** with the reader's understanding of the work.

4 = Adequately Competent
Sentences are **complete and generally correct**. There is evidence of a concerted effort to use a **variety** of structures.
Surface errors are present, but they **do not severely interfere** with the reader's understanding.

3 = Nearly Competent
Sentences are **generally complete and grammatically correct**, but there are errors that begin to distract the reader. Sentence structure might be accurate, but **dull or routine**.
Surface errors are **apparent** and **begin to interfere** with the reader's understanding of the work.

2 = Marginally Incompetent
Problems in **sentence structure** and **grammar** are **distracting**, and provide **little or no variety**.
Surface errors are **frequent and severe enough** to interfere with the reader's understanding of the work.

1 = Incompetent
Sentences are **riddled with errors**. There is **little or no variety** in sentence structure.
Surface errors are **frequent** and **extreme**, and **severely interfere** with the reader's understanding of the work.

Scoring Guide for the SAT Writing Test

WORD CHOICE

6 = Clearly Competent
The word choice is **specific, clear, and vivid**. Powerful nouns and verbs replace weaker adjective-noun/adverb-verb phrases. Clear, specific, and accurate words replace vague, general terms.
The work is **free of surface errors** (grammar, spelling, punctuation, etc.).

5 = Reasonably Competent
Word choice is **clear** and **accurate**. For the most part, the writer has chosen **vivid, powerful words and phrases**.
Sentences are **complete, generally correct,** and do not distract the reader from the flow of the discussion. There is evidence of a concerted effort to use a **variety** of structures.

4 = Adequately Competent
Word choice is **adequate**. For the most part, the writer has chosen **vivid, powerful words and phrases.**
Surface errors are present, but they **do not severely interfere** with the reader's understanding.

3 = Nearly Competent
Word choice is **inconsistent**.
Surface errors are **apparent** and **begin to interfere** with the reader's understanding of the work.

2 = Marginally Incompetent
Word choice is **generally vague** with a few attempts at vividness.
Surface errors are **frequent and severe enough** to **interfere** with the reader's understanding of the work.

1 = Incompetent
Word choice is **lazy, inexact,** and **vague**. The writer has either too limited a vocabulary, or has not sought the best words for the topic, audience, and purpose.
Surface errors are **frequent** and **extreme**, and **severely interfere** with the reader's understanding of the work.

Scoring Guide for the SAT Writing Test

HOLISTIC [1]

6 = Clearly Competent
The writing sample discusses the **topic effectively and insightfully**.

The paper is clearly **organized** around the central point or main idea. There is **sufficient** material (details, examples, anecdotes, supporting facts, etc.) to allow the reader to feel he/she has read a full and complete discussion without notable gaps, unanswered questions, or unexplored territory in the topic. Every word, phrase, clause, and sentence is **relevant**, contributing effectively to that idea.

The word choice is **specific, clear, and vivid**. Powerful nouns and verbs replace weaker adjective-noun/adverb-verb phrases. Clear, specific, and accurate words replace vague, general terms.

Sentences are **complete, grammatically correct**, and assist the reader in following the flow of the discussion. The use of a **variety** of sentence structures contributes to the effective organization of the work and the reader's understanding.

The work is **free of surface errors** (grammar, spelling, punctuation, etc.).

5 = Reasonably Competent
The writing sample discusses the **topic effectively**.

The **organizational plan** of the paper is **clear, but not fully implemented**. There is **nearly sufficient** material for a full and complete discussion, but the reader is left with **a few unanswered questions**. There is no superfluous or **irrelevant** material.

Word choice is **clear** and **accurate**. For the most part, the writer has chosen **vivid, powerful words and phrases**.

Minor surface errors are present, but they **do not interfere** with the reader's understanding of the work.

Sentences are **complete, generally correct**, and do not distract the reader from the flow of the discussion. There is evidence of a concerted effort to use a **variety** of structures.

[1]Adapted from materials appearing on www.collegeboard.com, the official website of the College Board.

4 = Adequately Competent
The writing sample **discusses the topic.**

The **organizational plan** of the paper is **apparent, but not consistently implemented.** There is **nearly sufficient** material for a full and complete discussion, but the reader is left with **a few unanswered questions.**
Word choice is **adequate.** For the most part, the writer has chosen **vivid, powerful words and phrases.**

Surface errors are present, but they **do not severely interfere** with the reader's understanding.

Sentences are **complete and generally correct.** There is evidence of a concerted effort to use **a variety** of structures.

3 = Nearly Competent
The writing sample **discusses** the **topic** but is **marred** by the following:

There is evidence of an **organizational plan,** but there are **too few** details, examples, anecdotes, supporting facts, etc.

Word choice is **inconsistent.**

Sentences are **generally complete and grammatically correct,** but there are errors that begin to distract the reader. Sentence structure might be accurate, but **dull or routine.**

Surface errors are **apparent** and **begin to interfere** with the reader's understanding of the work.

2 = Marginally Incompetent
The writing sample **discusses** the **topic,** but the discussion is **marred** by the following:

The **organizational plan** of the writing is obscured by **too few** details and/or **irrelevant** details.

Word choice is **generally vague** with a few attempts at vividness.

Problems in **sentence structure** and **grammar** are **distracting,** and provide **little or no variety.**

Surface errors are **frequent and severe enough** to **interfere** with the reader's understanding of the work.

1 = Incompetent

The writing sample **attempts** to discuss the topic but is **severely marred** by the following:

There is **no clear organizational plan** and/or **insufficient material.**

Word choice is **lazy, inexact,** and **vague.** The writer has either too limited a vocabulary, or has not sought the best words for the topic, audience, and purpose.

Sentences are **riddled with errors.** There is **little or no variety** in sentence structure.

Surface errors are **frequent** and **extreme,** and **severely interfere** with the reader's understanding of the work.